one

A FACE BEHIND THE NUMBERS

VADEN EARLE

PONDER
PUBLISHING

Ponder Publishing

15128 27b Avenue

Surrey, BC V4P 1P2

connect@ponderpublishing.ca

Design & Layout
Chad Aucoin, ICON Communications & Research Inc.

Editing Team
Cindy Stover, Christal Earle, Wanda Borely, Nicole Dufault,
Cathy Reid, Trisha Roberts, Meagan Tutti

Research Team
Cindy Stover, Natasha Hovey, Diane Ciarallo

Supporting Organizations
League Assets Corp., ICON Communications & Research Inc., Friesens,
Jet Blue Airways, Viva, Be a Hero, Hope for the Nations, FAZE Magazine,
Anti-Slavery International, World Vision, International Justice Mission.

ISBN:978-0-9737279-8-2
For Worldwide Distribution
Printed in Canada

This book is dedicated to every one person who has joined us on a Hero Holiday®, to every one person who has stepped out of their own comfort zone to identify with someone less fortunate, and to every one person who is surviving in an undesirable situation. These are the real Heroes of our day.

"A Hero is someone who understands the responsibility that comes with his freedom"

- Bob Dylan

Acknowledgments

Although my name is on the cover of this book, there is an army of people who have made this project come together. The staff at Absolute work tirelessly day in and day out to bring the ONE message to this generation. From travelling from coast to coast doing high school presentations, to organizing Hero Holidays®, to eighteen-hour office days, this team never quits. They are the unsung heroes who have given their lives to fight for those who do not have a voice. Thanks also to all the Hero Holiday® volunteers and crew... you make us want to dream bigger every year.

Absolute Board of Directors, we have stretched you, stressed you, and celebrated with you... thanks for all that you do and for believing in us!

Ralph and Sharon, Randy and Susan, Steve and Cathy, you believed in this vision and helped make it happen.

B-rad and the Kindness Crew, thanks for the great foreword.

Darian and the Ponder Publishing gang, thanks for the deadlines!

To Cindy and the editing team who lost much sleep because of this project, your extra hours have not gone unnoticed... you're all DPH's!

Terry and Chad at ICON, dudes... get some sleep, it's an hour later on the East Coast!

To Chad and the crew at Friesens, you guys rock! Thanks for all the patience!

Adam and Manny and the gang at League Assets Corp, you have no idea what we are going to accomplish together!

Jamie Mcintosh at International Justice Mission Canada. Get 'er done!

Chuck, Wood, Mole, Briss, Pipes, Gusi, Kint, Kehler, Nicholls, Johnson and Shley... enough said...

To my parents... thanks for adopting me. Good call!

To Bono, sorry, I've been so busy with this book that I haven't been able to take your call... but we should get together soon!

Finally, to my beautiful wife, Christal, the modern day "Mother Theresa." Your compassion for the poor has inspired me and hundreds of thousands of others!

Vaden Earle

"The curse of poverty has no justification in our age...
the time has come for us to civilize ourselves by the total,
direct and immediate abolition of poverty."

- Martin Luther King, Jr.

"The world desperately needs your voices."

- Stephen Lewis

Foreword

Have you ever been afraid of what the world has become?

We have all pondered how the world might become a better place. Each person I know has experienced that warm, fuzzy and motivating change-the-world feeling after watching an inspirational movie based on a true story. You know the one - an average person doing extraordinary things. After seeing it, most of us then say to ourselves, "Wouldn't it be something to be able to make a positive difference in the world? Just like that person in the film. Just imagine... think what it would be like!"

An enthusiastic conversation then continues, probably at a local coffee shop, on all the grandiose and infinite ideas that could save humankind. Inevitably, the evening ends with a statement, "If only someone would just do something."

I've heard it and I've said it. However, the next day, 99.9% of us go immediately back to our normal existence and awareness. Hoping, at best, that someone else is inspired to make the world a better place.

What stops each of us from rushing out to save the planet? Could it be a lack of faith in the power of ONE person being able to make a positive difference? Yet, few will bat an eyelash when agreeing about one individual's potential to hurt, murder, and destroy on a global scale. Logically, it must work both ways. If a small group of people can fly two planes into the Twin Towers of New York City, then I see no reason why another small group of people can't start a wave of kindness.

I've been asked the following question by 6-year-old students, 50-year-old CEO's, and even hosts from Good Morning America: "How does ONE person change the world?". The answer is always the same...

"Just choose ONE great idea and put it into action. Connect your passion and what you love doing, with what the world needs. Put your passion into action."

World-changing ideas are everywhere - they surround us every moment of our lives. But ideas are nothing without motivation and a sense of urgency. Try to determine what your personal motivation and sense of urgency are before you read this wonderful book. Write both down before you read chapter one. Everyone has a story, connect your own journey with those in this book. See through their eyes and you will never put off making a difference in the world we share.

After you read each chapter in this book, close your eyes.

Close your eyes and see all the great, world-changing ideas floating in front of you. Now, if you want to... you can actually reach out and grab any idea right out of the air.

Believe in yourself as you reach out your hand and clasp on to that world-changing potential. Hold that glimmer of hope in front of your face and truly look at it. Do not put the idea away, under no circumstance do you ever place that idea into your pants pocket. A pocket full of ideas is not something to be proud of. Make sure you put each great idea you have into action. Empty your pockets. Throw your ideas back into the world with love and purpose, see what happens.

Giving is not a sacrifice or an activity in place of enjoyment. Volunteering can be an adventure and a step towards a life less ordinary. It is ExtremeKindness, it is Absolute Leadership, it is Hero Holiday®, it is the act of being human. People are pre-programmed for kindness and helping others. It is the natural setting for each of us. The only time we ignore this preset response is when we feel that helping is another person's responsibility. Taking care of this world and the people in it, is an action that we must all commit to. For the first time in history there is now a global village with global problems; whether it be toxic lakes seen from space, the deaths of millions from AIDS, an iceberg melting too quickly, or a single child in Africa dying in the middle of the day on a crowded street. Each problem will have global ramifications. By ignoring our responsibility to make a positive difference, we give up our own future and the right to have one. There is no place to hide anymore; we must accept that we are no longer separate groups of race, creed or religion. Rather, we are one world and one people moving towards one tomorrow.

So all that's left to do is to grab an idea and be one.

B-rad Stokes
Co-Founder of The Kindness Crew
Co-Author of: Cool To be Kind, Call To Arms
www.extremekindness.com

Table of Contents

Child protection is paramount to this project.
All names and locations have been changed for
the protection of the children involved.

Photos appearing on the pages of this book
have no direct correlation to the stories that
accompany them.

Introduction

"I am only one, but still I am one. I cannot do everything,
but still I can do something."

- Helen Keller

Proceed with caution! The following pages that you are about to read may have a profound impact on your life. Most of us find it easy to live our lives against the backdrop of our own reality, but this book's goal is to challenge that reality. Not to challenge its validity as much as its broadness. Our view of reality here in North America is not incorrect, but it often is incomplete. The day of hiding behind that incompleteness is over. The information age is now making us accountable for the knowledge that we have access to. Africa is our neighbour; Cambodia is our friend; and Haiti, our brother. We can never again turn a blind eye and flippantly utter the words, "I never knew." Now we know.

The tattoo down my right forearm boldly displays the word JUSTICE, inspired by a nine-year-old Cambodian girl named Danya who was the near-victim of a North American sex tourist. I look at that tattoo every day as a reminder of why I get out of bed in the morning - of why I care. It reminds me of the night that I met Danya: the night my life was changed. Although the world is full of injustice, people need to consider the words of Helen Keller... "I can do something." Mother Theresa, Nelson Mandella, and Bono all have something in common. They did something. You may be one, but one can do a lot.

The purpose of this book is very simple: to introduce you to the one face behind each statistic, and to inspire that one person can do a lot.

As you read these few short pages, allow yourself to identify with the stories. Let your emotions take over. Try to put yourself in the shoes of the people featured. Cry, rejoice, yell, get mad; but above all, understand that there is hope. That hope lies in the hands of one person - that one person is you.

Where is Poverty?

On my list of eleven chapters, you may be surprised that "extreme poverty" does not get a mention. This isn't to say that poverty is not a problem, but rather that poverty is the key problem. All of the eleven issues that I have listed are often the result of extreme poverty. Here is the bottom line: end the poverty, begin to end the problems. People could stand up against corruption if they weren't living in desperation from day to day. Slavery would not exist if 'real' industry were a viable alternative. Parents would not sell their children if they didn't feel it was their only option.

Poverty kills.... and it must be stopped!

All things considered, the following eleven atrocities need to be talked about so that the world can become motivated to end this needless suffering. Don't get buried in the situations, get inspired by the possibilities!

Chapter 1

SLAVERY

intro

It is a good thing we abolished slavery...

It probably seems odd that a book written in this age would have a section on slavery. After all, that was a century ago, right? What most of us have failed to realize is that today, slavery is at its highest point in the world's history. Whether it be domestic house workers in Haiti, sex slaves in Eastern Europe or bonded labourers in India, the many faces of this atrocity are now covering the globe.

Slavery robs people of a basic human right: the right to be free!

Slavery robs people of their dignity! One of the ugliest things about this injustice is that it is often driven by the greed of those who already live in excess. Developing nations are working overtime to meet the consumer needs of "Western" society. With access to low-cost labour, retailers are forced to tap into foreign manufacturing or lose the competitive edge to the "big box" super stores. More often than not, this means slavery.

For many people, the image that comes to mind when they hear the word slavery is the Transatlantic Slave Trade. We think of the buying and selling of people, their shipment from one continent to another and the abolition of the trade in the early 1800's. Even if we know nothing about the slave trade, it is something we think of as part of our history rather than our present. But the reality is slavery continues TODAY.

Millions of men, women and children around the world are forced to lead lives as slaves. Although this exploitation is not often called slavery, the conditions are the same. People are sold like objects, forced to work for little or no pay and are at the mercy of their 'employers'. [1]

Photo: Justine Armstrong

Photo: Stephanie Hunter

4

'Recently, my wife and I visited one of the children that we sponsor in Thailand.

In preparation for the trip, we looked for gifts that we could bring for our child and his family. As we made our way through the sports section of a local discount store, my eye caught sight of a soccer ball. This was a good quality, brand name ball, selling for just eight dollars. Not a bad deal! I hate the thought of giving a sub-par gift, so this find was particularly special to me. Once we arrived in Thailand and the moment approached to give out our gifts, I reached into my backpack to retrieve the ball, and my heart sank as I read, 'Made in Thailand',

This ball had potentially been manufactured by children younger than its eager recipient.

...and then shipped to Canada where it sat on the shelf of a sporting goods store, which no doubt, sold dozens of that same model for exorbitant prices. When the season was over, it was shipped off to the discounters, where it finally caught my attention in a bargain bin. At this point I returned it to it's homeland and into the hands of a young impoverished Thai boy.

Soccer is the world's favourite sport. Dirt-poor fans all over the earth pay small fortunes to watch some of the world's richest people kick around a ball hand-stitched by children. In Pakistan, a recent study discovered that there are more than 15,000 children in Pakistan being used to stitch footballs. In India, it is suggested that upwards of 10,000 children were being used for this same purpose. Meanwhile, the sporting goods industry claims to know of only 70 child labourers doing this kind of work. [2]

Shawna. When she was 7, she was living with her very, very poor family in a village
a. Her mother was giving birth to her baby brother and needed about $25 to pay
doctor. The only way they could get $25 was from the local moneylender, who
nded that the family sell Shawna to him. She was made to roll cigarettes by hand
ys a week, 12 hours a day, sitting in one place on the floor. If Shawna didn't roll
cigarettes a day, she was beaten. She was paid about six cents a day.

hree years, when we met her at 10 years of age, she was not one penny closer to
g off her debt. This is bonded slavery. While it is illegal in India, we believe there are
15 million children in such circumstances there, rolling cigarettes, making jewelry,
ng fireworks, and breaking rocks with little hammers.

> - Gary Haugen, Founder, International Justice Mission

years is nothing. Haugen's International Justice Mission (IJM) freed a man
was a child when he took a debt of $4.00, 58 years ago! His children had been
ved for their whole lives, toiling to help their father pay off that minuscule debt. "It
andemic, affecting several areas of the world." IJM and other worthies are fighting
ng hope in a hopeless situation.[3] World Vision reports that "60% of all children in
cities are full-time wage earners. Child prostitution is one of the principal means
aking money."[4] In Africa, estimates are that 25 percent of the children between the
of 10 and 14 are involved in labour.[5]

126 million children around the world are in work that is harmful to their health and welfare. [6]

Photo: Stephanie Hunter

Photo: Aili-Anne Newstead

10

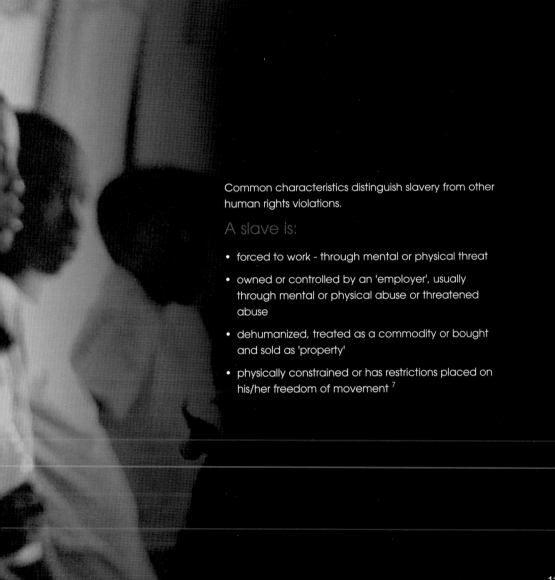

Common characteristics distinguish slavery from other human rights violations.

A slave is:

- forced to work - through mental or physical threat
- owned or controlled by an 'employer', usually through mental or physical abuse or threatened abuse
- dehumanized, treated as a commodity or bought and sold as 'property'
- physically constrained or has restrictions placed on his/her freedom of movement [7]

"They buy something I suffer to make."

The most infamous scandal of the early third millennium was coined "The Chocolate Slaves." On May 4, 2001, BBC News reported that the Ivory Coast government blamed international chocolate companies for artificially sustaining low cocoa prices, and, in so doing, forcing some farmers in poverty to use child slave labour.

More than 90 percent of cocoa from The Ivory Coast is procured by the sweat of child labour, according to "Slavery", a documentary broadcast on British television. When the documentary filmmakers asked the former slave, known as Victor, if he had ever tasted chocolate, he said "no." When they asked him what he would say to the millions of Britons who ate chocolate daily, Victor answered: "If I had to say something to them it would not be nice words. They buy something I suffer to make." [8]

"No one shall be held in slavery or servitude; slavery and the slave trade shall be prohibited in all their forms."

- Article 4, Universal Declaration of Human Rights

"Slavery... I didn't know about all these forms that existed. I think it's largely because we aren't expecting it. It is hidden. Generally people would not believe that it is possible under modern conditions. They would say 'No, I think you are making it all up', because it's just too incredible..."

- Archbishop Desmond Tutu, Hull, UK, 1999

Photo: Aill-Anne Newstead

13

Bonded labour affects millions of people around the world. People become bonded labourers by taking, or being tricked into taking a loan (under exorbitant interest), for as little as the cost of medicine for a sick child. To repay the debt, many are forced to work long hours, seven days a week, up to 365 days a year. They receive basic food and shelter as 'payment' for their work, but may never pay off the loan, which can be passed down for generations.

Forced Marriage
Early and forced marriage affects women and girls who are married without choice and are forced into lives of servitude often accompanied by physical violence.

Forced labour
Forced labour affects people who are illegally recruited by individuals, governments or political parties and forced to work - usually under threat of violence or other penalties.

Slavery by Descent
Slavery by descent affects people who are either born into a slave class or are from a 'group' that society views as suited to being used as slave labour.

Trafficking
Trafficking involves the transport and/or trade of people - women, children and men - from one area to another for the purpose of forcing them into slavery.

Photo: Stephanie Hunter

15

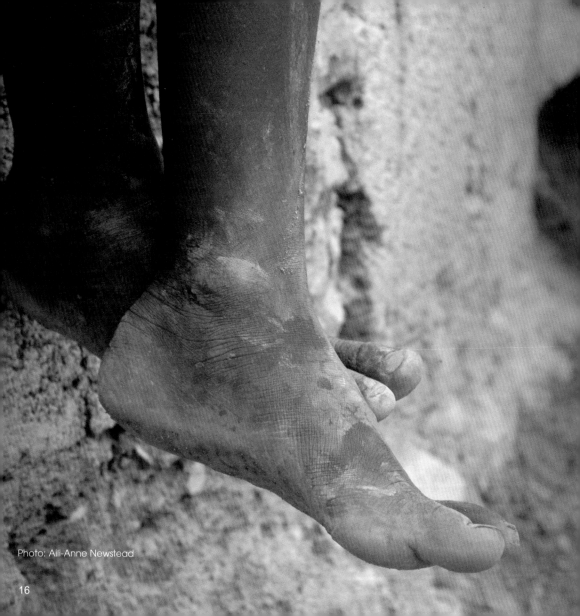

Photo: Aili-Anne Newstead

Sridhar lives in southern India. When he was 10 years old his family sold his labour to a local moneylender so they could buy necessities to live. His freedom was sold for 1,500 rupees (approximately $31.00 USD) and for a year, Sridhar spent the day sitting on a dirt floor rolling cigarettes. He was required to complete a minimum of 1,000 cigarettes a day, 6 days a week and was paid a meager 10.00 rupees a day (approximately 20 cents), which was far below the legally-required minimum wage.

Sridhar reported that he was beaten with a stick by the moneylender if his quota was not met.

His debt had to be repaid to the moneylender in a lump sum, which would be impossible since Sridhar's family desperately needed the money to live and buy food, and the moneylender forbade Sridhar from working for anyone but him until the debt was repaid. It is through this system that many children are bonded, grow to adulthood still working to pay off their debt, and eventually pass this same debt onto their children. It is a vicious cycle that is virtually inescapable for impoverished families.

In July 2001, investigators with the International Justice Mission learned of Sridhar's slavery and after determining that he was illegally bonded, helped him fill out an affidavit that was submitted to local government officials. Sridhar was released from his debt and was then able to go to school, no longer spending his days rolling cigarettes.[10]

Despite the fact that bonded labour is illegal in most of the countries where it is being practiced, governments are rarely willing to enforce the law, or to ensure that those who profit from it are punished.

Today millions of people in the world are in bonded labour. [11]

"Bonded labourers are non-beings, exiles of civilization, living a life worse than that of animals, for the animals are at least free to roam about as they like. This system, under which one person can be bonded to provide labour for another for years and years until an alleged debt is supposed to be wiped out, which never seems to happen during the lifetime of the bonded labourer, is totally incompatible with the new egalitarian socio-economic order which we have promised to build."

- Justice PN Bhagwati,
Indian Supreme Court, 1982

"Child labour has serious consequences that stay with the individual and with society for far longer than the years of childhood. Young workers not only face dangerous working conditions. They face long-term physical, intellectual and emotional stress. They face an adulthood of unemployment and illiteracy."

- Kofi Annan, Former United
Nations Secretary-General

19

Photo: Stephanie Hunter

This is Shankar, a 6 year old boy in bondage in Bangladesh:

I was very small and I am still small. I used to have to handle the heavy instruments to cut the knots in each carpet. Many times, my thumbs and fingers were injured when the cutter slipped. Then I would cry for my mother, but the Master would only beat me. He never took me to the hospital or gave me any medicine. What he used to do was, take a match stick (grind the tip into powder) and fill the cut with the match stick powder then he would set fire to it with another match so that my skin and blood would bond together. I would cry for my mother, and he would beat me again. [12]

There are more people in slavery right now than in 4 centuries of the Transatlantic Slave Trade combined... we thought that was only in history!

- Kevin Bales, Director of Free The Slaves [13]

In Pakistan, brothers Mohen and Nihal began working on carpet looms when they were four and five years old in order to help their family meet their basic needs.

"The health hazards caused to us are that our fingers are trimmed and we have to work all day long. Often for a couple of days in a week, we have to work for the whole day and night. Mohen often gets miserable and fatigued with the long hours of work and he tries to escape. Then the master weaver keeps a strict watch on him and never lets him move for three or four days." [14]

"I was scared... if I made a mistake I was beaten with a stick."

When Ahmed was five years old he was trafficked from Bangladesh to the United Arab Emirates to be a camel jockey. He was forced to train and race camels in Dubai for three years.

"When I said I wanted to go home I was told I never would. I didn't enjoy camel racing, I was really afraid. I fell off many times. When I won prizes several times, such as money and a car, the camel owner took everything. I never got anything, no money, nothing; my family also got nothing."

Ahmed was only returned home after a Bangladesh official identified him during a visit to Dubai in November 2002. A local NGO provided him with the specialist support and help he needed to resume his life with his family. [15]

Photo: Stephanie Hunter

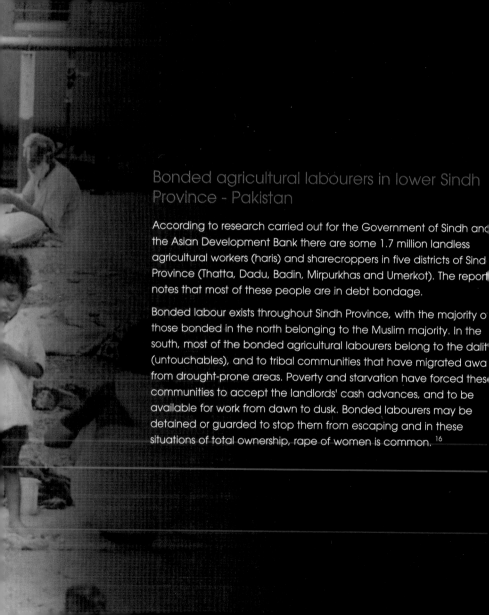

Bonded agricultural labourers in lower Sindh Province - Pakistan

According to research carried out for the Government of Sindh and the Asian Development Bank there are some 1.7 million landless agricultural workers (haris) and sharecroppers in five districts of Sindh Province (Thatta, Dadu, Badin, Mirpurkhas and Umerkot). The report notes that most of these people are in debt bondage.

Bonded labour exists throughout Sindh Province, with the majority of those bonded in the north belonging to the Muslim majority. In the south, most of the bonded agricultural labourers belong to the dalit (untouchables), and to tribal communities that have migrated away from drought-prone areas. Poverty and starvation have forced these communities to accept the landlords' cash advances, and to be available for work from dawn to dusk. Bonded labourers may be detained or guarded to stop them from escaping and in these situations of total ownership, rape of women is common. [16]

bonded labourers work for no wages, with the food and clothing provided being
to their debt. Along with interest payments on the loan, this increases their debt
aily basis. Most are forced to provide 'begar', a form of forced, unpaid labour, on
he tasks assigned against the debt. Trafficking of bonded labourers who are
to pay their debts is a common practice among landlords. Bonded labourers are
one landlord to another, usually for a price higher than the debt they had with
evious landlord thereby increasing the bonded labourer's debt again. [17]

od deal for who?

onducting on-site investigations and interviews with Chinese workers at Wal-Mart
es in China, the National Labour Committee issued a report describing the abysmal
ent of workers at such manufacturing plants. One particular section of the report on
n Shi handbag factory describes:

our shifts, 7 days a week, 30 days a month

age take-home pay of 3 cents an hour, $3.10 for a 98-hour workweek

worker earning 36 cents for an entire month's work

ercent of the workers earning nothing at all and actually in debt to the company

ers held as indentured servants, with identification documents confiscated, only
ved to leave the factory 1 hour a day

workers fired for fighting for their basic rights. [18]

case you're one of those people who think that even $3.10 for a week's wages is
otable in 'those countries', - you're wrong! Basic necessities such as food, water and
s to health care are unattainable with these wages, regardless of 'the country'. I am
ggesting that the wages of a developing nation should be standardized to the level
ustrialized nations. But they do need to be culturally relevant, and not oppressive to
dividual. All too often the workers in these factories are receiving wages that are in
on to their basic human rights.

To this day, every country in the Western World continues to reap the benefits of slavery.

Chapter 2

HUNGER

intro

I'm starving!

We have all said it. Even something as insignificant as a tiny craving can often push us to utter those words. The unfortunate truth is that there are people in the world that are hungry... millions of them. Not the kind of hunger that makes you order pizza in the middle of the night but the kind of hunger that makes you wonder if you are going to live past next week. Imagine the turmoil of being a parent and having to choose which of your four children to feed today. What about being a 12 year old boy knowing that your 5 year old sister cannot eat unless you steal?

These scenarios embody what the word injustice really means.

Sometimes I wonder what hungry people in the developing world would say if they knew how picky we can be about what we eat here in the West. Can you imagine a hungry child in Ethiopia turning up their nose at a meal because they simply "do not like" something on their plate? The thought would never cross their mind, yet we can always find a way to complain about what we have, no matter how excessive it might be.

Photo: Stephanie Hunter

31

Photo: Augusto Rosales

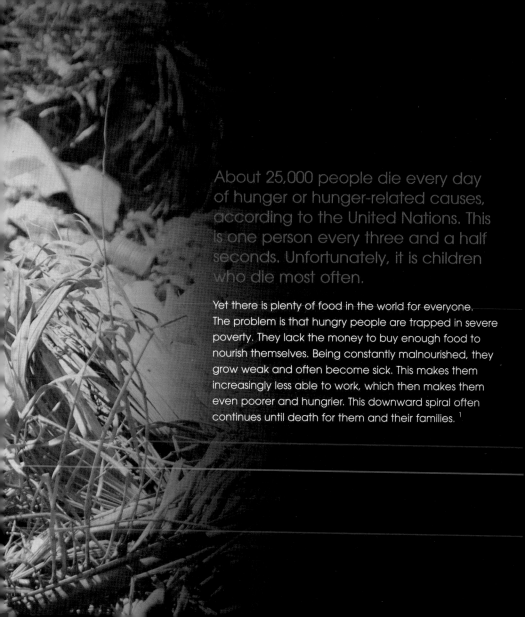

About 25,000 people die every day of hunger or hunger-related causes, according to the United Nations. This is one person every three and a half seconds. Unfortunately, it is children who die most often.

Yet there is plenty of food in the world for everyone. The problem is that hungry people are trapped in severe poverty. They lack the money to buy enough food to nourish themselves. Being constantly malnourished, they grow weak and often become sick. This makes them increasingly less able to work, which then makes them even poorer and hungrier. This downward spiral often continues until death for them and their families. [1]

Poverty keeps hungry people from buying enough food to nourish themselves. Poverty keeps sick people from receiving basic medical treatment or taking simple preventative measures. The vast majority of these preventable deaths occur among the poorest people in the poorest countries.[2]

Countries in which large portions of the population battles hunger daily are usually poor and often lack the social safety nets we enjoy; such as soup kitchens, food stamps, and job training programs. When a family that lives in a poor country cannot grow enough food or earn enough money to buy food, there is nowhere to turn for help.[3]

Essentially, hunger is the most extreme form of poverty. Individuals or families cannot afford to meet their most basic need for food. The problem is that famine and starvation are not the only ways that hunger becomes a factor. Most poor people who battle hunger deal with chronic undernourishment and vitamin or mineral deficiencies, which result in stunted growth, weakness and heightened susceptibility to illness. [4]

Photo: Augusto Rosales

35

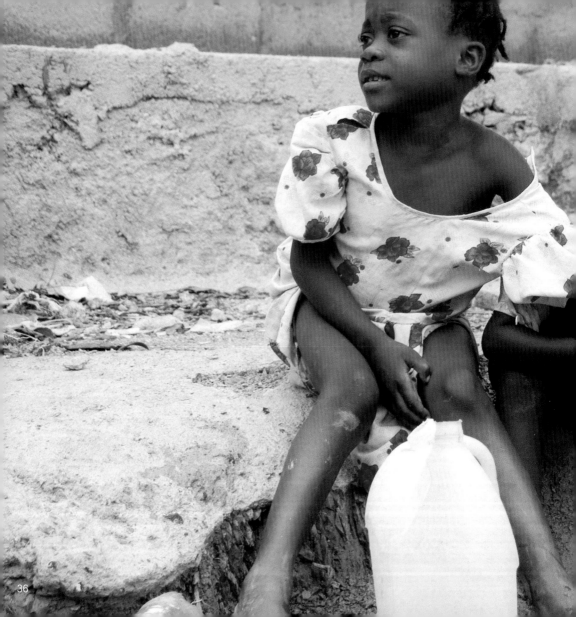

In areas of extreme poverty, it is common for children to eat dirt to try to make the hunger pains stop.

Photo: Augusto Rosales

I met Jillianna in a red light district in Dominican Republic. I was there with two philanthropists showing them how desperate the situation had become in this area. The goal, of course, was to garner financial support for development projects in that region. Given the nature of where we were, we were being accosted by prostitutes every few minutes; then Jillianna emerged. She spoke better English than most people that we met that night and she was clearly feeling out of place. As I engaged her in conversation, it became increasingly clear that she was not a "prostitute" as we would define it. She lacked the sensual swagger and the seductive poses. She truly looked awkward in that situation.

I asked Jillianna why she was there, but I was not prepared for her answer. With a sheepish look on her face, she uttered these words:

"What I do is very bad. I am not proud of myself, but my mom is dead and my dad is very sick. My little sister lives with us and she has a baby. I am responsible for paying for the house and the medical care of my father. I also have a little boy of my own... and he is always hungry..."

He is always hungry. Those words haunt me to this day. How is it that the Western world can justify getting fat on our excess, while moms are forced to have sex with strangers because their children are hungry?

Photo: Justine Armstrong

40

Most of the world is laden with need; much of it desperation.

One of the biggest problems facing the West is a lack of purpose.

Why can we not bring these two worlds together to help each other?

Not My Turn

A priest working in Africa watched a little boy he knew named Zachary playing all day with twigs underneath a tree. Eventually the priest wandered out to see Zac, on the way picking a mango from the tree for him.

While they chatted, the boy played with the mango. Finally the priest said to Zac: "Well go on, eat it." Zac replied: "I can't Father, it's not my turn to eat today." That little boy was living the reality of many people in the poorest countries who have so little food that they have a rotation to decide who eats on which day. [5]

43

Consider this... today our world houses 6.55 billion people.

854 million people across the world are hungry.

Economically, the constant securing of food consumes the valuable time and energy of poor people, allowing them less time for work and earning income.

In 2005, about 10.1 million children died before they reached their fifth birthday. Almost all of these deaths occurred in developing countries, 3/4 of them in sub-Saharan Africa and South Asia, the two regions that also suffer from the highest rates of hunger and malnutrition.[6]

In the developing world, 27% of children under 5 are moderately to severely underweight.

In the United States, approximately 61% of the population is overweight.[7]

Photo: Stephanie Hunter

Photo: Stephanie Hunter

46

Worlds Collide

Recently, a friend of mine who is an aid worker, returned from the field to Canada to raise some project support. A common friend of ours invited her to hear a popular television preacher who was in the area for one night only. Because of the nature of her work abroad, they managed to get her a front row VIP seat to hear this televangelist speak. This particular preacher was known for his ability to raise large amounts of money, so she thought that she might gain some tips from the event. It didn't take long for her to realize that she was out of place in that gathering. The speaker went into a 45 minute explanation about how wealthy he was. He even went so far as to say that he had a climate-controlled garage built for his Harley Davidsons because he didn't want them to experience more than a five degree flux in temperature. She obviously did not stick around.

As she was telling me this story, I asked her what went through her mind at that moment. She answered very quickly.

"The names of my friends who have been forced to put their children on a feeding schedule where each kid gets to eat every four days."

Developed countries have, for the most part, overcome hunger, and overconsumption is now a much greater problem than lack of food. [8]

There are nearly one billion people in the world that are hungry, and one child dies of hunger related causes every 3.5 seconds.

Chapter 3

TRAFFICKING

intro

There are many atrocities in the world today, but perhaps none are as vile and offensive as child trafficking. The depravity of the human race has somehow allowed people to think that selling other people for personal gain is acceptable. The apparent fact is, many Westerners consider themselves to be more valuable than those who live in the developing world. It is this mindset that lends itself to all kinds of injustice.

When the topic of Human Rights comes up in the Western World, it is often in the context of greed or opportunism. People are quick to cite their nation's constitution or charter of rights when it comes to gaining an advantage. Labour disputes and strikes seem to inevitably fall under the umbrella of human rights when people want higher wages and better work conditions. However, have you ever heard of a Westerner fighting for a basic human right, such as the right to not be bought or sold as a commodity?

It may seem redundant to have a chapter about Trafficking in a book that already has one on Slavery. These two topics, however, have some very distinct differences. Yes, trafficking is indeed a form of slavery. Yes, slavery can, and often does, include trafficking. I feel, however, that the topic of Trafficking deserves some special attention because it is one of the world's fastest growing and most lucrative industries.

Consider it this way: Slavery is the act of holding a person in labour against his or her will. This can be as complex as the child labour situation or as simple as a family member being held as a household servant. Trafficking is the transporting or selling of a human being into slavery. This always involves deception and often crosses international borders.

According to Anti-Slavery International, trafficking is more about the act of transporting the person and less about what happens at the final destination.

Increasingly, children are also bought and sold within and across national borders. They are trafficked for sexual exploitation, for begging, and for work on construction sites, plantations and domestic work. The vulnerability of these children is even greater when they arrive in another country. Often they do not have contact with their families and are at the mercy of their employers. Human trafficking involves the movement of people through violence, deception or coercion for the purpose of forced labour, servitude or slavery-like practices.[1]

People should never be the property of other people. Please move forward with caution. The content of this chapter is not for the faint of heart but it is a reality and it needs to be talked about.

Photo: Stephanie Hunter

Photo: Stephanie Hunter

My introduction to the issue of human trafficking came when I read the following story in the book *Be a Hero*. If we can't think of any other reason to be involved in advocacy and action, stories like this one are reason enough.

Sukan will break your heart. She is an eight-year-old Cambodian girl, sold by her parents to help pay the expenses of raising the rest of their family. Spirited out of Cambodia into Thailand along with another little girl, she was sold again. New "owners" and a false passport got the two to Toronto's Pearson International Airport and through customs. After a day of pornographic photography, they sat on a stool and watched a dozen white men pull out cash from their wallets and pass it to their "owner." The two who ponied up the highest amount got the honour of deflowering the two virgin children.

After being robbed of their childhood by the two wealthiest men, the little girls were subjected to a series of rapes lasting through the night. The next morning they were taken across the Windsor border into the United States. Stripped, each was given a number on her back right shoulder blade with a black felt marker and pushed into a large room behind the stage in a club. They weren't alone. Sukan and her partner were overwhelmed by the sight of nineteen 8-10 year olds, all naked, all numbered with the black felt marker. This night was to be a slave auction.

After being paraded out in a cattle call, and submitting to a litany of instructions: "jump, turn, bend over, strike alluring poses", they were herded backstage. Then each was brought out alone to be auctioned off. Sukan was reserved for the end. She'd been told that the health of her family and her own future prospects hinged entirely on her performance. She determined to excel. She danced, hopped, twisted and turned like her very life depended on it. A heated bidding war escalated as Sukan tried even harder spiralling, arching, bending, smiling anything to increase her value. Finally the auctioneer called those time-honoured words "going once, going twice, sold!"

"Sukan's eight-year-old life was hawked for forty-two thousand dollars - the highest price ever paid for a prostitute at this site." [2]

Trafficking is a global problem affecting
every continent and most countries.

54

It occurs within and across national borders and ranks as one of the most lucrative forms of international crime.[3]

Photo: Augusto Rosales

55

The story of 'Id' is typical of the hardship these children experience. Now 15 years old, he has returned to Mali after two years, having been trafficked to work on a coffee and yam plantation in the Ivory Coast.

'Our day began at 5am. Carrying heavy tools on our head, we had to walk six kilometres through mud and stones in bare feet to reach the fields. By the time we reached them we were soaked through and exhausted. Once we arrived, the overseer showed us the area we each had to plant before the day's end. We were afraid of what he would do to us if we could not finish the work. This threat and the threat of being denied food if we could not finish in time forced us to work quickly. The work was hard and bending all day gave us back pains. If we were ill and couldn't work we were afraid that we would be tortured to death. One day I witnessed two of my colleagues being tortured for trying to escape. They became seriously ill and died.' [4]

Photo: Augusto Rosales

57

trafficking is slavery because traffickers use violence, threats, and other forms of coercion to force their victims to work against their will. This includes controlling their freedom of movement, where and when they will work and what pay, if any, they will receive. [5]

Photo: Augusto Rosales

When Ellen was 17 she was abducted by a group of men in Albania and taken to a flat where she was held for two months. During this time she was beaten and raped. Then a man came and made arrangements for them both to go abroad. At the time Ellen thought she had been rescued, but her new 'boyfriend' was another trafficker who took her to the UK where he forced her into prostitution. She had to see between 15 and 40 customers a day and give the money to her trafficker. When she tried to refuse, she was beaten.

After about a year she was picked up in a police raid. She did not say anything to the police because her trafficker had told her not to and she was worried about getting her family into trouble. She was held at Heathrow airport for two days, while immigration officers arranged to have her sent back to Albania. No arrangements were made for her to be seen by an NGO in the UK or after she arrived back in Albania.

Ellen went back to live with her family, but received threatening phone calls in the early hours of the morning. Her family wanted her to go to the police, but Ellen did not trust the police in Albania.

Concerned for herself and the safety of her family she decided to let the traffickers take her back to the UK. A few months after she was trafficked to the UK for the second time, she managed to escape from her trafficker. She made an application to stay in the UK, but this has been rejected by the Home Office. [6]

In 2005, the International Labour Organization estimated at least 2.4 million people have been trafficked. [7]

UNICEF now believes that the number of children trafficked annually is around 1.2 million. [8]

Photo: Augusto Rosales

61

Pia is a firecracker! A feisty little girl who is so forward and outgoing that it made me a little nervous. One night we were joking and chatting when she brought up the topic of the foreigners that have been helping her mother out. One of them even built her a small house just outside the city. This 'nice man' did all of this in exchange for the rights to a young girl. It is sad that this mother has the responsibility to care for her children but is simply unable to do so. When he would come to town, he retained the right to take Pia or either of her sisters to his hotel room for up to a week at a time.

Pia came and lived with me in my program for a little while. She was incredibly difficult because she had no concept of rules, no concept of the need to be quiet at a certain time, going to bed on time, not stealing food or fitting into any sort of program. These kids are so hard to work with when they're from the streets. Most rescue programs want kids that are respectful, successful and cleaned up. They want the easy cases; the kids that are nice, polite and grateful for the help. I would love to find some of those kids but, more often than not, the kids that you get to work with are hard - they are cold and they're jaded.

And so Pia ran away from my program one night. I spotted her downtown; she was still selling flowers. The minute she saw me, she ran away. As she meandered her way through a maze of dilapidated shacks, I finally caught up to her. "Jenni I think that you're going to be angry at me and I'm sorry, I'm sorry, I'm sorry." I reassured her that she had no need to be sorry, nor did she need to hide from me. I told her that I loved her even if she never came back to the program again and that I would do everything in my power to protect her.

Pia still sells flowers; she still sells her body. I know for a fact that she also prostitutes her younger siblings. She's a 14-year-old Madame. I don't hate her for it; I don't despise her for it. I don't think it's possible to because she is a child who is broken. She is a child who is in pain; she is a child who is hurt.

Just think about this cycle of abuse that we let go on because we don't punish violators enough. We don't call for this kind of behaviour to stop. We victimize the children. We say to the children who are prostituting themselves, "well, they must like it; they must enjoy it," but I don't think she does. I think this is all she knows. This is the only way she knows how to be. It is difficult to watch that. She's now 17, working in a massage parlour where she is doing almost anything but massages. It would be very easy to consider her a failure. I think many people have given up on this sweet little one, but I know we can't. 60% of the girls that we work with are going to end up back on the streets and in the same situations that they came from.

Every time I go back to visit, Pia is one of those that come running up the street screaming "Jenni, Jenni!" She'll bury her head in my chest and just be held there and be offered love with no expectations. I don't want anything from her. I just want her to know she's loved and cared for and someday she will succeed, I know it. Someday she will, but it's hard to wait for that someday.

- Jenni Kornell, Viva Network

Photo: Augusto Rosales

Photo: Stephanie Hunter

It is estimated that two children per minute are trafficked for sexual exploitation.[9]

In 2004, between 14,500 and 17,500 persons were trafficked into the United States.[10]

Human trafficking generates between 10 and 12 billion dollars a year for organized crime.[11]

Some 120,000 women and girls are trafficked into Western Europe every year.[12]

The illicit profits from human trafficking is second only to the trafficking of drugs.

Shuvaloy Majumdar is Deployment Leader of The Future Group, a Calgary-based non-profit organization fighting the sex trade. While based in the Cambodian capital of Phnom Penh, Majumdar brought Susan McClelland, of Maclean's Magazine, to Svay Pak to show her the scale of the child-sex trade. In Susan's words... He leans out his window and lies, telling a boy he wants a girl much younger than those on the street. Majumdar knows that children as young as four are hidden by their pimps in an attempt to avoid police raids.

Inside, Majumdar takes a seat in a creaky metal chair beside a stained mattress. Within seconds, two girls, who claim they're 6 and 8, join him. Just awakened, they're wearing cotton pajamas and rubbing the sleep out of their eyes. At first, the girls stand silently and rigidly together. The pimp slaps one on the back of the head and the girls begin to awkwardly and unenthusiastically flirt with Majumdar. Shaking, the 6-year-old mumbles, "no boom-boom, just ngam-ngam," (Vietnamese slang for oral sex). But when a photographer who has accompanied Majumdar begins to take some pictures, the pimp and his bodyguards draw guns, thinking Majumdar and the photographer are undercover informants. Thinking fast, the visitors defuse the situation by telling the angry pimp the pictures are for their business - organizing sex tours out of Thailand. The ruse works and the danger passes.[13]

Trafficking equals convenience for the perpetrators.

Pedophiles can now book their holidays online. Choosing the child that they abuse is as easy as choosing an airline or hotel.

"Today's Internet has also become the new marketplace for child pornography."

- U.S. Attorney General John Ashcroft.[14]

67

Newsweek recently reported that in 2000, the Chinese government crackdown caught dozens of traffickers and freed 110,000 women and 13,000 children.[15] Some 200,000 children are trafficked every year in West and Central Africa. These children are employed on fishing vessels and farms, in prostitution and sweatshops.[16] The number of trafficked children being intercepted at the Benin border has risen from 117 in 1995 to 1,081 two years later. In 1997, Benin police arrested five West Africans caught preparing to ship 90 child slaves to Gabon after they had bought the youngsters in Benin and Togo for as little as $1.50 - the cost of a coffee. The situation is so bad that CNN reports that on April 17, 2001, UNICEF spokesman Alfred Ironside asserted, "The slave trade never stopped in West Africa."[17]

Ra Ratt is a frail 14-year-old whose vagina has been stitched up more than five times so that clients would think she was a virgin. Her owners forced her to take clients well before her wounds healed, so that the men would believe that the bleeding was from her torn hymen.

"It was so very painful," she said with a shudder. Last year, she followed a neighbour from her home in Preah Vihear, 200 km north-east of Phnom Penh, to look for work in the city to help her mother, three sisters and brother. Her father had died.

In the city, she was left in a house with promises that work at a restaurant would begin the next day. But that evening, she found she had been sold for US $1,000.

For a year, she saw many clients - Koreans, Japanese, Singaporeans, Malaysians, Taiwanese, and Caucasians. "I cannot remember most of them - as soon as one leaves, another comes in," she said. She worked from 8:30 A.M. to 10 P.M. and there were beatings if she could not meet the quota of clients. Often, she was taken to a doctor who would put her under anaesthesia and stitch up her vagina. [18]

Characteristic methods of trafficking:
- kidnapping
- coercion (debt payment for home, family, travel, etc.)
- abuse - physically and emotionally
- personal threats or threats to harm family members
- identity theft

Even the widely accepted practice of domestic servitude
lends itself to a cycle that often results in trafficking.
Consider the following article by Anti-Slavery International:

The International Labour Organization estimates that domestic work is the largest single employment category of under 16-year-old girls in the world. Although the numbers that this represents are not known, it is likely to run into the millions worldwide. The majority of children in domestic labour are between 12 and 17, but in many countries children routinely begin working as domestics well before 12 years. Child domestic workers routinely suffer discrimination, a loss of freedom, identity and self-esteem and denial of schooling. They are also vulnerable to physical and verbal abuse and suffer from the effects of the work that they do and the conditions under which they do it. Sexual exploitation of child domestic workers due to the child's vulnerability and isolation in the homes of their employers is common. They are accepted sexual outlets for the men or boys of the household. In cases where the girls become pregnant they are often thrown out of the house and are forced to fend for themselves on the streets, since the shame of their situation makes it difficult for them to return home. Many families reject these 'spoiled girls' because 'their behaviour' has brought dishonour to the family. In these instances, domestic work typically becomes a precursor for prostitution, as the young girls have few other options available. Traffickers of children into the sex trade routinely deceive children and their families about what will happen to them by promising them attractive jobs as domestic workers. In other cases evidence suggests that the exploitation of trafficked children can be progressive, meaning that children who have been trafficked to work as domestics may later be forced into prostitution. Children trafficked across borders to work as domestics are often discarded or abused by employing families. They then have little choice but to turn to prostitution as a means of survival in a foreign country with no means of returning home. [19]

Photo: Stephanie Hunter

Sex trafficking has now been internationally
defined as terrorism.

Chapter 4

ORPHANS

A child should never be alone.

Since the beginning of time, parents have had the responsibility of caring for their children. It is natural for a parent to nurture and provide for those that they bring into the world. From the smallest, most insignificant member of the animal kingdom to the wealthiest of people, this instinct is built right into who we are.

Unfortunately, poverty, disease and war have infiltrated the very essence of this basic law of nature. A great injustice in the world today is the plight of the orphan.

A five-year-old girl in Uganda should not have the responsibility of caring for herself. A nine-year-old boy in Iraq should not have to work to earn money to feed his little brother. A child should never be alone.

It is hard to decide what seems more tragic: the pains of hunger or the pains of a child's loneliness. This chapter addresses the very difficult topic of orphans. Amidst all the other things that this book deals with, there is something so wrong about the thought of a child being abandoned. The previous chapters and those that follow are primarily dealing with issues that have some sort of physical effect on the child. Although orphans often end up dealing with those issues as well, there is a level of emotional trauma that is associated with the feeling of abandonment.

Photo: Jamie-Lee Burton

Approximately 12 million children in Africa
have been orphaned by AIDS.[1]

Photo: Stephanie Hunter

79

Teddy lives in a village in southern Uganda. Her parents died of AIDS-related illnesses when she was eleven. She now lives with her three brothers and sisters and helps to look after three other boys whose parents also died of AIDS-related illnesses.

"My mother and father died in 1996. My father died in the hospital. But I saw my mother die here. Because I was a bit older than the others, I looked after her. I used to cook food for her, wash her clothes, and boil herbs for her. She told me she was suffering from AIDS, but she didn't tell me how she got it or how to avoid it. I wish she'd told me more about it. I'd like to know how it's transmitted. When my mother died we suffered so much. There was no food, and there was no one to look after us. We didn't even have money to buy soap and salt. We wanted to run away to our other grandparents, but we didn't have transport to go there. I tried to be positive, but it was difficult. I missed my mother because I loved her so much. When my mum was here we didn't suffer. We had food and money for buying things. Some neighbours say bad things about us: "Those children are so poor; they don't even have relatives. They don't belong. They don't have a clan." Some people also call us 'AIDS orphans', and they say that maybe our parents infected us. We don't say anything. At least no one oppresses us. We're also free to play when we want, and there's nobody telling us to do this or that."

A while ago some neighbours came here and asked us to sell them our trees. We agreed and we sold them. But they haven't given us the money. We've tried getting the money from them, but they won't give it. Sometimes people come and steal food from our garden. My grandfather's brother comes and takes the coffee. He just steals it when the beans are still on the trees. I don't go to school. I'd like to go, but my grandparents and neighbours told me to stay at home and look after the others. If I were educated I'd like to be a nurse. I want to treat other people and heal them from whatever they're suffering from. I want to do this because when my mother was sick, there was nobody to look after her because we had no money.[2]

Now he knows he is loved...

I think it was love at first sight. I met him at a garbage dump, and his story broke my heart. He was an orphan who had been without parents for more than 7 years. When I asked him his name, he responded with a statement that changed my life: "I can't remember what my mother called me." How could this be possible? How do children like this exist in this world? In that moment, I experienced a new resolve that has come to redefine my life and values. Five days later, as our truck pulled once more into the village where we had been working for the past month, I was immediately scanning all the beautiful little faces looking up at me and searching for my special one. I saw him within a moment because he was trying to catch my eye and a huge smile crossed his face as soon as I waved. I jumped out of the truck and we came running toward each other. His laughter was infectious as I smothered him with kisses and love.

The medical team and the Hero Holiday® students that had come with me that day all set up their clinic and braced themselves to see over 100 people in a 3 hour time period! After everyone got settled into their routine, I grabbed the hand of my little friend and we stole away so I could quietly give him the gifts and tell him about the surprise I had for him. We went to a quiet place with two other orphaned boys and I brought out their gifts. Their eyes filled with excitement as I brought out shiny basketball jerseys and some rice and beans, and the brand new can of Pringles chips for each of them! They were so excited! They kept asking, "for me?" and I was choking back the tears as I saw their eyes when I handed them their new clothes. I could tell that they had never owned anything so nice before and the whole moment seemed almost holy and surreal to me as we stood in this dirty alley and shared such an intimate experience. I pulled my little friend aside, bringing my translator to help me. I told him how much I loved him and how special he was. I told him that I had thought for a long time about a name for him and I wanted to give him something special that would remind him all the time of how much he was loved. I had searched for a meaningful name and I had found the perfect one: David, because 'David' means to be loved and cherished. His eyes lit up and I asked him if he understood that. He nodded his head and as I kissed him through my tears, I saw a little tear in his eye. I held him and told him that from now on, whenever we saw him, we are going to call him David so he is reminded of how much he is loved. He nodded his head and hugged me.

As I tell David's story, I often want to cry; but this is about more than emotion and it is about more than sympathy or even empathy. It is about love. Love is the highest human aspiration. Is not the goal of all to love and be loved? When I look at David, I see love.

Every moment we have to make a difference has the possibility of leaving a resounding impact through to the generations to come. Our lives are an amazing gift and the best possible thing that we have to offer is our own willingness. In David's village, there are 36 orphans. All of them are displaced people with no citizenship. They are enslaved by poverty, and some of them that I have met were physically enslaved and exploited before they got there. They have escaped violence and abuse, and are currently still very vulnerable and needy. They need education and they need people like me and people like you to see their cause as our own. We succeed when they succeed.

Yesterday, we went back to David's village, and my friend John walked up to him. When he looked at him, he pointed and asked "David?" and David broke into a huge grin and pointed at himself and said, "me!". Who would have ever thought I could find something so beautiful and valuable in a garbage dump? He is my treasure!

- Christal Earle - Co-Founder of
  Absolute Leadership Development

Photo: Augusto Rosales

83

Photo: Erin Smart

When we first entered the building, a sense of awe came over the crowd. The screams, crying, chaos and smells were nothing less than an all-out assault on the senses. What else can you expect from a tiny renovated warehouse that houses nearly fifty abandoned orphans? With most of these kids being mentally or physically challenged, this place has become a bit of a 'last chance' children's home. high needs children are often an added emotional and financial burden to their parents, especially in third world settings where resources are limited. This orphanage hosts a number of children who have been abandoned by their families with no one in the world to care for them. This is the story of Louis, as told by one of his care workers:

We have many interesting stories here but one of the most powerful is that of Louis. Seven months ago, we received a call from a local newspaper. They got a report that an abandoned child was found in the garden in front of the hospital. When the authorities got there, they found Louis. A six year old boy, Louis was crying and shivering alone in the garden. He was not healthy but he was alive. Once we brought him back to health, we realized that he had sustained considerable brain damage. Everybody thought that Louis would be nothing more than a vegetable. As the months passed, Louis became more and more responsive and we discovered something fascinating. Although Louis was unable to talk, he understands several languages fluently. Deep inside that broken body lies a brilliant little man who's hug can brighten the darkest of days.

"Home is where the heart is." Where does this leave those who have no home? It is sad when unfortunate circumstances or poor choices leave a man or woman without a home. It is tragic, however, when an innocent child is forced to live on the street for no reason other than their place of birth.

At least 150 million children worldwide are believed to live at least part of the time on the streets. [3] "The present day numbers of street children in single cities like Calcutta may be equal to the total population of those cities in the 19th century." [4]

Homeless children in Brazil number around 12 million.[5] That is a city the size of Mexico City nearly filled with homeless children!

Enkhbold, now 10, lived on the streets for more than three years. Enkhbold's mother left when the children were young. His father was imprisoned for theft. Enkhbold, aged 6, and his sister, aged 13, ended up running away. He was wandering alone on the city streets, cold and bored, when another boy asked him to join his group in an underground tunnel. Enkhbold was the youngest and smallest of the 10 children in the tunnel so they nicknamed him 'Youngst.' Although the tunnel was cramped, dark and stinking, it was still the best option for him. Enkhbold made a living by begging and using the money to buy bread and ice cream, and sometimes a candle to light his way in the tunnel. One winter's day, social workers from World Vision provided the group with hot meals. Soon they asked if he would like to live in the street children's centre. Enkhbold thought, "I don't know what the centre is like, but as I do not like living in this hole, I better go with them." So he did and the Light House became his new home. [6]

Photo: Stephanie Hunter

Dressed in a small pink shirt, he had his head buried into the arm that was holding his weight against the corner of a bleak concrete wall. No older than three years old, he was sobbing incessantly, his chest heaving in utter anguish. He looked and sounded as if he were about to hyperventilate at any moment.

This was Abrahim's first day at the second institutional orphanage we visited in Iraq.

His mother had left him at ten days old. His father left him yesterday. He was abandoned on the outskirts of the town during temperatures soaring to almost 50 degrees Celsius. His two young sisters were discarded at the same time, during the same blazing heat.

Everything Abrahim knew, everything he identified as being his life, everything he held as being normal and secure, changed in an instant.

I'm sure I've been at many orphanages and orphan homes on the day that children were brought there for the first time. However, I've never been consciously aware of it during the 200 or so such places I've visited over the years. This was right in my face... and right through my heart.

To experience the very moment of gut-wrenching pain, loss, questioning, betrayal, change, destruction of self esteem, crushing of worth... was to also wound my own soul.

I wish that I could say that Abrahim will now find a new sense of belonging and a new sense of family but, sadly, that is hardly ever the case within a government-run orphanage. [7]

Photo: Stephanie Hunter

Africa has the greatest proportion of children who are orphans. In 2001, 34 million children in sub-Saharan Africa were orphans, one-third of them due to AIDS. Because of AIDS, the number of orphans is increasing dramatically. By 2010, the number of orphans will reach 42 million. Twenty million of these children - or almost 6 percent of all children in Africa -will be orphaned due to AIDS.

Asia has the largest number of orphans. Due to Asia's large population, the number of orphans in Asia is much larger than in Africa. In 2001, there were 65 million orphans, with approximately 2 million of them orphaned due to AIDS. The populations in many Asian countries are so large, however, that even at a low prevalence, the number of people with HIV/AIDS threatens to surpass the numbers in some of the most severely affected African countries. Even a relatively small increase in prevalence could lead to even greater numbers of orphans due to AIDS.

Orphan populations are concentrated, reflecting broader trends in HIV prevalence and population. In 2001, 12 countries in sub-Saharan Africa accounted for 70 percent of the orphans. The three countries with the largest populations also had the most orphans - Nigeria, Ethiopia and the Democratic Republic of Congo. However, the impact of AIDS will be felt even more acutely in countries with smaller populations, but higher HIV prevalence rates. In addition, within countries, orphan populations vary greatly based on the concentration of HIV prevalence.

The number of orphans will continue to rise. Today's prevalence rates will largely determine the pattern of orphaning for the next decade. In countries where HIV/AIDS prevalence has recently escalated, the full impact on the estimated number of orphans has yet to emerge.[8]

Sometimes she forgets for hours at a time. On the weekends, she sits with her friends from school. They braid each other's hair in fancy spiral patterns, and look at Bollywood film stars in a scavenged magazine, and paint each other's toenails (delphinium blue is all the rage). Then Tigist feels like a kid, like all the other kids.

But when it's coming on dusk and she walks back home, when she takes the jerry can to the standpipe around the corner to buy water, puts a few pats of cow dung to burn in the brazier and boils a small pot of lentils - when she calls her brother, Yohannes, in from the street and chides him about his homework - then the illusion crumbles. After Yohannes falls asleep sprawled on their one narrow bed, and she has nudged him over to make room for her own arms and legs, then she lies in the dark and runs through the list. Is there money for their rent? Is there money for their fees at school? Is there money for more lentils, more dung, more water? And just where, exactly, is she going to find the money for another sweater for Yohannes, because his wrists now dangle four inches below the cuffs of the one he has?

"I shouldn't be worried about this," Tigist said to me. She spoke without bitterness or rancour - simply to make clear that she knew what she had lost. "It should be for others to worry."

Ten or fifteen years ago, it wouldn't have been up to Tigist: someone would have stepped forward to take care of an orphaned ten and six-year-old when their mother died. It would have been as unthinkable in Addis Ababa as it would be in Toronto or Dallas or Birmingham for two small children to set up house on their own. But in the age of AIDS, the net of family and community that once caught and cared for children such as these has frayed and finally unravelled altogether.

Well over twelve million children across Africa have been left without parents because of AIDS. These children can't go to school if no one pays their fees, and many end up either struggling to grow food on land they have never been taught to farm, or living wild on city streets. Aid agencies express fears about the cost to countries of a generation growing up without education or even socialization, and alarmed political leaders talk about orphans as a threat to national stability. What these children need is parents, and no cash infusion, no matter how great, permits a country such as Ethiopia to buy parents for 700,000 AIDS orphans.[9]

Photo: Stephanie Hunter

Chipo Baloyi's mother and father both died of AIDS. At only 17, Chipo is responsible for the welfare of herself and five younger siblings, aged 7 to 13. She somehow manages to take care of her family in a country where families and communities can barely fend for themselves, much less care for the growing number of AIDS orphans.

Chipo's family had to sell all its livestock to care for - and then bury - her dying father. Nine months later, her mom fell victim to the same "strange, unnamed" disease.

Zimbabwe has the dubious distinction of having the world's highest rate of HIV infection, at 25 percent. One of every five children there has lost one or both parents to HIV/AIDS.

"There are now very few families in the country that have not been affected directly or indirectly by AIDS," says Patrick Makokoro, project development officer with Mercy Corps Zimbabwe.

"Many families in Chipo's village have lost loved ones to AIDS, but because of the stigma associated with the disease, people do not discuss what caused their deaths."

It takes a village to raise a child.
It takes a global village to raise 50 million orphans.

Chapter 5

HIV//AIDS

intro

Imagine your life this way.

You get up in the morning and have breakfast with your three kids. One is already doomed to die in infancy. Your husband works 200 miles away, comes home twice a year and sleeps around in between. You risk your life in every act of sexual intercourse. You go to work past a house where a teenager lives alone tending young siblings without any source of income. At another house, the wife was branded a whore when she asked her husband to use a condom, beaten silly and thrown into the street. Over there lies a man desperately sick without access to a doctor or clinic or medicine or food or blankets or even a kind word. At work you eat with colleagues, and every third one is fatally ill. You whisper about a friend who admitted she had the plague and whose neighbours stoned her to death. Your leisure is occupied by the funerals you attend every Saturday. You go to bed fearing adults your age will not live into their 40s. You and your neighbours and your political and popular leaders act as if nothing is happening. [1]

One of the most tragic things about the AIDS pandemic is that it has gone unresolved for two generations. Sadly, it has taken a backseat to other crises in the minds of many people in the West. It is almost like we have gotten comfortable with the idea that this one is not going away. We have adopted such a bizarre sense of familiarity with this monster that we sometimes forget that it even exists. It appears that there is no more shock factor with AIDS. We have all heard the numbers and simply cannot be shocked anymore. Could it be that the sting has worn off, and we've moved on to a different tragedy?

How can it be that millions of innocent deaths can become normal? The fact remains that HIV/AIDS is the deadliest plague of our modern age. The senselessness is that it's now largely treatable, but corruption and economic policies are not allowing us to get the medicine to the frontlines.

It has been said that history will remember our generation for two things: the advent of the internet, and our response to the AIDS crisis. It is time for us to wake up and respond appropriately.

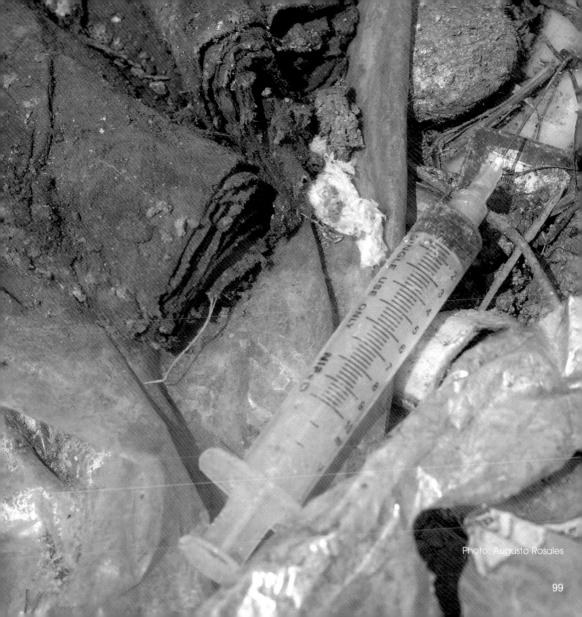

Photo: Augusto Rosales

Photo: Augusto Rosales

There are nearly fourteen million children who have lost one or both parents to AIDS. It is predicted that there will be more than twenty-five million of them by 2010. This is a tragedy of enormous consequence. AIDS is killing more people than were killed by all of the worst wars of history and natural disasters.

AIDS is a war against humanity.

What we talk about, and the actions we take, must be influenced by the fact that this is a war, which requires mobilization of the entire population. These children will grow up without the love and care of their parents, and most of them will be deprived of their basic rights - shelter, food, health and education. Many will be subjected to abuse, violence, exploitation, discrimination, trafficking, and loss of inheritance. We have an obligation to provide the proper care and support for these children. No adult should stand by and watch while these children suffer. [2]

This year, more than half a million babies in the developing world will contract from their mothers the virus that causes AIDS, despite the fact that drugs and therapies exist that could virtually eliminate mother-to-child transmission of the killer disease.[3]

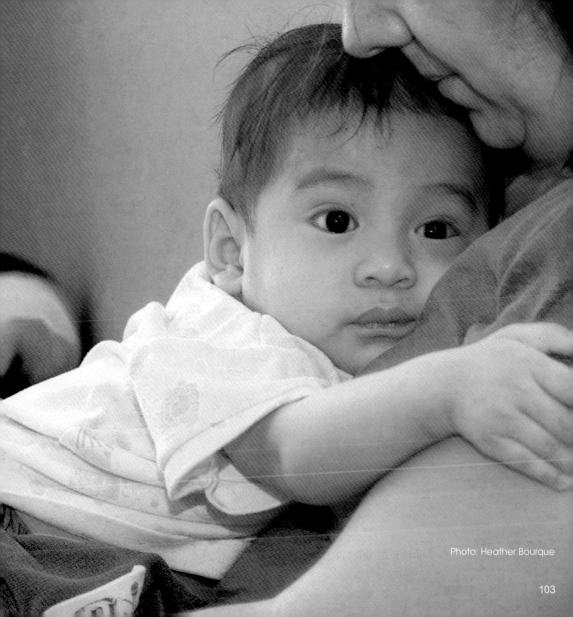

Photo: Heather Bourque

103

6,500 Africans are still dying every day of a preventable, treatable disease, for lack of drugs we can buy at any drugstore. This is not about charity, this is about justice and equality.

Because there's no way we can look at what's happening in Africa and, if we're honest, conclude that deep down, we really accept that Africans are equal to us. Anywhere else in the world, we wouldn't accept it. Look at what happened in Southeast Asia with the Tsunami. 150,000 lives lost to that misnomer of all misnomers, 'mother nature.' In Africa, 150,000 lives are lost every month. A tsunami every month. And it's a completely avoidable catastrophe.

It's annoying, but justice and equality are mates. Aren't they? Justice always wants to hang out with equality. And equality is a real pain.

- On The Move - Speech by Bono [4]

Photo: Justine Armstrong

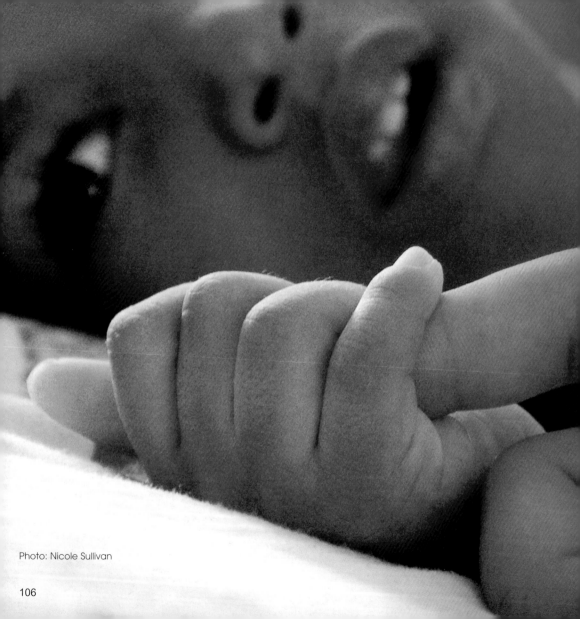

The sight was shocking. Peering into the medical ward of Queen Elizabeth Hospital was like peering into a corner of hell. AIDS has overtaken the hospital. Seventy percent of the medical-ward admissions are AIDS-related, but the hospital lacks the proper medications to treat the sick. So the patients come to die in ever increasing numbers, far beyond any capacity to manage.

Two to a bed; sometimes three to a bed. When the beds overflow, the next wave of the dying huddle on the floor under the beds, to stay out of the way of the families, nurses, and doctors passing through the wards.

The constant low-level moans and fixed gazes of emaciated faces fill the ward. These patients are dying of poverty as much as they are dying of AIDS. In the next corridor is an outpatient service that offers AIDS drugs. Four hundred or so patients are successfully being treated with antiretrovirals. They are the tiny fraction who can afford to pay approximately $1.00 per day out of pocket for the medicines.[5]

"Every day lost is a day when ten thousand more people become infected with HIV. We can beat this disease, and we must."

- Kofi Annan, The 7th Secretary - General of the United Nations

"From my perspective, the mesh of poverty and HIV/AIDS is the deadliest combination on the planet, and there's not the slightest possibility of confronting poverty so long as AIDS runs its savage course."

- Stephen Lewis, Former UN Special Envoy for HIV/AIDS in Africa [6]

Photo: Augusto Rosales

AIDS is now second only to the Black Death as the largest epidemic in history. AIDS kills about 2.9 million people a year, which is approximately one person every 11 seconds, as you can see here. This death toll surprisingly includes a lot of children, who are often infected with the HIV virus during pregnancy or through breast-feeding.

The toll is worst in Africa, where millions of parents have died, leaving children as orphans. Often teachers have died as well, leaving schools empty. Doctors and nurses have died, leaving hospitals and medical clinics with nothing. Farmers have died, leaving crops in the fields. Entire villages have been devastated.

Yet AIDS is a preventable and increasingly treatable disease. The huge majority of deaths can be stopped. Through education, the use of condoms, and proper medicine, AIDS has been brought under control in the developed countries. The same can be true in Africa and other poor areas of the world. [7]

Yufa leans against the pink neon-lit doorway of a café. She's a farm girl who has been in the sex game for only two weeks. She's wearing an ill-fitting red gown, and her feet hurt. Her pale, exposed shoulders are a sharp contrast to her face, burnt from labouring in fields. She came from Sichuan to look for factory work in Urümqi after her young husband died, leaving her with two children "and only the sky overhead," she says. In Urümqi, there were no jobs. A stranger fixed her up at a roadside brothel where she sells herself for $3. "Sure, I know about the disease," she says. "But I'm not so pretty, and I only get maybe three clients a week. If they won't use a condom, fine. I'll do it anyway. What choice do I have? I can't let my children die of hunger." [8]

Fallen Sick...

- The spreading HIV/AIDS epidemic has quickly become a major obstacle in the fight against hunger and poverty in developing countries.

- Because the majority of those falling sick with AIDS are young adults who normally harvest crops, food production has dropped dramatically in countries with high HIV/AIDS prevalence rates.

- Since the epidemic began, 25 million people have died from AIDS, which has caused more than 15 million children to lose at least one parent. For its analysis, UNICEF uses a term that illustrates the gravity of the situation; child-headed households, or minors orphaned by HIV/AIDS who are raising their siblings.

The social and economic impacts of AIDS threaten the well-being and security of millions of children worldwide.

As parents and other family members become ill, children take on greater responsibility for income generation, food production, and care of family members. They face decreased access to adequate nutrition, basic health care, housing, and clothing. Fewer families can afford to send their children to school, with young girls at particular risk of being denied an education. In both urban and rural areas, many orphans are struggling to survive on their own in child-headed households. Many others are forced to live on the street. [9]

Photo: Stephanie Hunter

113

Elijoy weighs no more than a porcelain tea pot. Her tiny face alternates between expressions of pain and alarm, a range that neatly covers not only her own situation, but that of her country. Elijoy is two months old, born in an isolated village in the highlands of Lesotho. Her mother died two weeks after Elijoy's birth of what was most certainly AIDS. For two weeks, relatives kept Elijoy alive on water, before carrying the featherweight bundle of baby down from the hills and turning her over to her maternal grandmother, Esther. Esther knew the child was desperately ill, and wanted to take her to hospital, but this presented her with an anguishing dilemma: her granddaughter needed doctors at a clinic in one direction, but she needed to see doctors in another. Esther has AIDS, and is one of only a few thousand in Lesotho on anti-retroviral (ARV) treatment. Her stock of drugs was running low and she needed to travel several hours to one of the few treatment centres to have it replenished. She couldn't leave the baby, but she had to get those drugs.

In the end, she brought the baby to a Christian mission, and staff from a new Médecins sans frontières project took the unusual step of giving her enough ARV tablets to tide her over so she could stay to tend to the child.

Little Elijoy's problems are not so easily solved: the odds are high that she too has been infected with HIV, but she can't be tested accurately until she is at least six months old. Meanwhile, she is so malnourished, and generally miserable, that it is hard for the staff at the Scott to know where to begin. "There it is: three generations with AIDS," one doctor said, gesturing at the baby.

"That's what's happening in this country. Three whole generations." [10]

Photo: Heather Bourque

"One hundred thousand," he said.

I bounced in the passenger seat and endeavoured to keep the disbelief out of my voice as I asked if he was sure.

"One hundred thousand, more or less." In a lifetime of driving the pitted highways of East Africa, Mohammed reckoned he had had sex with 100,000 women.

I tried to do the quick calculation on whether that was even possible. He was forty-eight. He had started driving at eighteen. Could a person have sex with 100,000 women in thirty years? And still have time to work? Or eat?

I met Mohammed at a truck stop outside Nairobi in mid-2005. I had long been interested in Africa's long-haul truckers, the tens of thousands of men who move most of the goods on the continent. Their transient lives have made them key players in the spread of HIV, and I was hanging around in the dust, looking for a trucker who might let me ride with him for a while and get a sense of his life.

Truck drivers are vilified all over the continent for spreading HIV - and there is some truth in the accusation. Long-haul truck drivers such as Mohammed have an HIV infection rate that is roughly twice that of the general population. And they remain a key group for the transmission of the disease: because they have what is, by regional standards, a good income; because they spend most of their lives in environments where sex is bought and sold and little social stigma is attached to these transactions; and because many truckers, like millions of others on the continent, have refused to modify their sexual behaviour in the face of frightening evidence of the risks involved.

"There are so many women on the road and they are very tempting, the way they dress is very alluring... and these women are in business - they know marketing. They show you a piece of cake and they are ready to serve it, so there is no problem buying it. You look at her and immediately you start doing the calculation, How can I get her?"

There are no condoms in the bars or lodges, and Mohammed said he has never seen them available anywhere on the routes he drives. Until a few years ago, he had no idea that Africans even used them; he thought they were a strictly foreign phenomenon. The lack of condoms reflects the tension between the conservative cultural and political environment and the reality of the pandemic. Sex with prostitutes causes an estimated 40 percent of HIV infections in Kenya. Yet here and elsewhere in sub-Saharan Africa, sex workers are rarely included in national AIDS plans.

Mohammed said he had heard about the disease over the past decade, and knew that it was transmitted by sex. He had been feeling flu-like symptoms for some time, and when he went for a test in November 2003, his sole motivation was to "set a good example."

"What did the test say?" I asked? "Positive?" He nodded. "It was a very big shock," he acknowledged. "But I took it very easy because I'm a truck driver and I could die at any time." Mohammed wasn't sure when he had been infected - obviously, there was no shortage of opportunity.

"Do you worry about getting sick?" I asked him.

"Yes," he said. "But everybody dies one day." [11]

Photo: Stephanie Hunter

I have spent the last four years watching people die. Nothing in my adult life prepared me for the carnage of HIV/AIDS... the pandemic feels as though it will go on forever. The adult medical wards of the urban hospitals are filled with AIDS-related illnesses, men, women, wasted and dying;

aluminum coffins wheeling in and out in Kafkaesque rotation;

...in the pediatric wards, nurses tenderly removing the bodies of infants; funerals occupying the weekends, cemeteries running out of grave sites; in the villages, hut after hut yields a picture of a mother, usually a young woman, in the final throes of life. No one is untouched. Everyone has a heartbreaking story to tell. Virtually every country in East and southern Africa is a nation of mourners... I have to say that the ongoing plight of Africa forces me to perpetual rage. It's all so unnecessary, so crazy that hundreds of millions of people should be thus abandoned. [12]

"The situation is dire. We must act now. And we cannot remain indifferent to the devastating toll that the AIDS epidemic is taking. Those of us that live in affluent countries have the moral responsibility to do something and work together."

- Michaelle Jean, Governor General of Canada

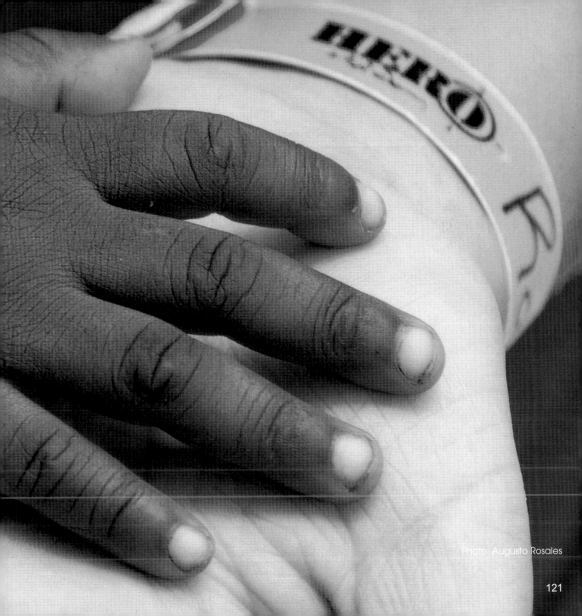

Photo: Augusto Rosales

AIDS treatment can cost as little as 30 cents a day,
yet only 30% of those infected have access to it.

Chapter 6

intro

Oil. Greed. Power. Pride. Land. Money.

Has there ever been a war in history that didn't begin with one of these at the top of the agenda? At what point do we justify the loss of human life as a means for personal or national gain?

The facts are very simple. War kills more innocent women and children than it does soldiers.

This chapter, more than any other, has the overwhelming potential to be very political. Without expressing a personal opinion on any specific conflict, my goal in this section is to paint a realistic picture of the cost of war. Not in terms of dollars, barrels of oil, or territories conquered, but rather in terms of humanity. Who are the people that really pay the price for the conflict?

"I believe all suffering is caused by ignorance."

- Dalai Lama, 1989 Nobel Prize speech

126

Human Rights Watch records the testimonies of the traumatized survivors of Congo's horror - which is, in itself, traumatizing and dangerous work. Human rights activists have been abducted, tortured, and murdered.

In late 2002, a Pygmy man told this story: About 20 miles from Mambasa, the militia attacked a pygmy camp. A man called Amuzati who was hunting in the forest heard shooting. As he wasn't far from his camp he returned to see what was happening.

About half a mile away from the camp he heard shouts and crying, and then there was silence. He came closer and saw several militiamen.

He saw the corpses of his family, including his nephew who was five years old, with his stomach cut open. They were cutting the flesh and eating the victims.[1]

Not surprisingly, "scores of millions have been scarred psychologically by the violence they endured or witnessed at intimate range, and countless others have died for lack of food or health service." [2]

Consider the words of one child soldier...

"They beat all the people there, old and young. They killed them all, nearly 10 people... like dogs they killed them... I didn't kill anyone, but I saw them killing... the children who were with them killed too... with weapons... they made us drink the blood of people, we took blood from the dead into a bowl and they made us drink... then when they killed the people they made us eat their liver, their heart, which they took out and sliced and fried... and they made us little ones eat." [3]

Susan, sixteen years of age, captures the brutalization children suffer at the hands of the Lord's Resistance Army (LRA) in northern Uganda in the following testimony: One boy tried to escape but he was caught. His hands were tied and then they made us, the other new captives, kill him with a stick. I felt sick. I knew this boy from before; we were from the same village. I refused to do it and they told me they would shoot me. They pointed a gun at me, so I had to do it... I see him in my dreams and he is saying I killed him for nothing, and I am crying.

The emotional scars of war are more difficult to measure. A nationwide survey of 3,000 children in Rwanda in 1995 revealed the following: over 95 percent of the children witnessed massacres; over a third had seen family members murdered; almost all believed they would die; nearly two-thirds were threatened with death; and over 80 percent had had to hide to protect themselves, many for up to eight weeks or longer. And even those who've survived war have persisting threats to life and health. In 64 countries, an estimated 110 million anti-personnel mines lie in wait for unsuspecting footfalls. These cost between $3 and $10 to buy and between $300 and $1,000 to remove. About 800 humans die every month because of them, with thousands more maimed for life.

It is more than just numbers:

"I've seen people get their hands cut off, a 10 year old girl raped and then die, and so many men and women burned alive. So many times I just cried inside my heart because I didn't dare cry out loud."

- Grace, 14-year-old girl, abducted by a
rebel group in Sierra Leone [4]

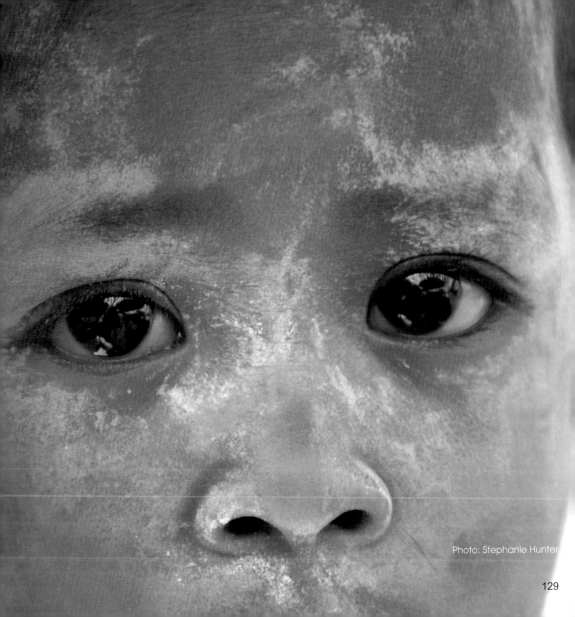

129

The lyrics of the following song were written about teen depression but could easily be the cry of a child in a war torn nation. The bottom line is many of the children in these situations have lost hope of any sort of change.

There's nothing to lose when no one knows your name. There's nothing to gain but the days don't seem to change.

Nothing To Lose - Billy Talent

Driven from their homes...

"The people who lived in this camp for displaced people had already been driven from their homes by government troops and Janjaweed (militiamen), but the government of Sudan decided to attack them again. In the middle of the night, the government of Sudan bulldozed the camp to send a message to the residents. The message: non-Arabs are not welcome here." [5]

Photo: Stephanie Hunter

ANTI-FLAG LYRICS - "*Anatomy Of Your Enemy*"

It is very interesting to hear this band's take on war propaganda. The following is a summary of what they call "the ten steps to create an enemy and start a war." Although they are writing these words from a particular political slant, they bring an interesting point to light. Much of the media surrounding war is based on ignorance toward the opposing culture. In fact, most people do not fear other people, they fear the unknown.

1. Create the enemy. Sometimes this will be done for you.
2. Be sure the enemy you have chosen is nothing like you. Find obvious differences like race, language, religion, dietary habits, fashion. Emphasize that their soldiers are not doing a job, they are heartless murderers who enjoy killing!
3. Once these differences are established, continue to reinforce them with all disseminated information.
4. Have the media broadcast only the ruling party's information. This can be done through state run media. Remember, in times of conflict all for-profit media repeats the ruling party's information. Therefore all for-profit media becomes state-run.
5. Show this enemy in actions that seem strange, militant, or different. Always portray the enemy as non-human, evil, a killing machine.
6. Eliminate opposition to the ruling party. Create an "Us versus Them" mentality. Leave no room for opinions in between. One that does not support all actions of the ruling party should be considered a traitor.
7. Use nationalistic and/or religious symbols and rhetoric to define all actions. This can be achieved by slogans such as "freedom loving people versus those who hate freedom." This can also be achieved by the use of flags.
8. Align all actions with the dominant deity. It is very effective to use terms like, "It is God's will" or "God bless our nation."
9. Design propaganda to show that your soldiers have feelings, hopes, families, and loved ones. Make it clear that your soldiers are doing a duty; they do not want or like to kill.
10. Create an atmosphere of fear and then offer the ruling party as the only solution to comfort the publics fears. Remember the fear of the unknown is always the strongest fear.

Photo: Stephanie Hunter

War has taught me to place my trust in peace, and I believe that all citizens of the world deserve the right, and the opportunity, to live without violence. I believe it will be possible, some day, for war - and all the death, destruction, and unfathomable hardship that war brings - to be a footnote in the history of humankind. At the very least, I believe, it is incumbent upon us to try.

- Dr. Samantha Nutt - Founder of War Child Canada

For nearly twenty years, the Ugandan government has been involved in armed conflict with the rebel group called the Lord's Resistance Army (LRA). The LRA has a particularly ugly way of replenishing its ranks: kidnapping.

Their targets are children between the ages of eight and fourteen.

Rebels raid villages, stealing what they need and burning the rest. According to UN estimates, more than thirty thousand children have been forced into the service of the LRA since 1994. [6]

Kamal is a young man of 22. He is lying on a bed in the intensive care ward after having undergone surgery on his left leg. His arms and his face are heavily burnt; he is covering the scars with a towel while he speaks:

"I am from Baghdad. My job is to work as a guard for a security company. About two weeks ago, we were travelling from the north towards Baghdad in a convoy to deliver goods. I was sitting on the first car, a pick-up-truck. Suddenly there was an explosion. I went unconscious. When I woke up I saw the driver of my car lying next to me - he was dead. The other two men in the car were also wounded. They brought us to this hospital. I have several fractures in my left leg and these burns on my face, my arms and my side. In total, 22 percent of my body surface was burnt. I had surgery on my leg. All in all, I am happy I am still alive. When I get out of the hospital I will continue to work as a guard. Life has to go on!" [7]

Said, 30, is another patient of the ward:

"I am from a small town near Mosul. Five days ago I was walking with my cousin in the streets. Suddenly there was heavy machine gun-firing in our direction. I was hit by several bullets on my right side. I was in big pain. My cousin, who was not hit, brought me to this hospital, where I underwent surgery. The doctors promised that in some days I could go home. In my town I own a gas station, but now I don't want to continue working there.

When you are in the street you never know when a bomb or a car might explode next to you.

We always knew that one day or another something like this could happen to us. We have always expected it. I have a wife and eight children. I tell them to stay at home and not come and see me. It is too dangerous to be on the roads. I am in a constant worry about my family. But what can we do, this is our life." [8]

Landmines kill or maim at least one person every hour... more than 100 million remnants of conflicts, past and present, lie quietly in the ground, waiting for action.

One in every 236 Cambodians is an amputee - and they're the lucky ones. Surgeons from the International Committee of the Red Cross assume that up to half of mine victims die instantly or bleed to death, unable to reach medical care in time.[9]

Although the following numbers are not recent, the message is loud and clear. When a nation is in war, its people suffer.

In 1992 and 1993, the GCMHP surveyed 2,779 Palestinian children between the ages of 8 and 15 and found the following staggering information:

- 93% had been tear-gassed
- 85% had their homes raided
- 55% had witnessed their father being beaten
- 42% had been beaten
- 31% had been shot
- 8% had a brother imprisoned
- 9% had been detained
- 3% had suffered a death in their family
- 63% were exposed to more than four different types of trauma [10]

There are about 300,000 child soldiers involved in over 30 areas of conflict worldwide, some even younger than 10 years old. Child soldiers fight on the front line, and also work in support roles; girls are often obliged to be sex slaves or "soldiers' wives". Children involved in conflict are severely affected by their experiences and can suffer from long-term trauma. [11]

Photo: Stephanie Hunter

Yousif is my niece's son. He is 12 years old. Two weeks ago, while they were having a family gathering in Baghdad, terrorists attacked their house.

They killed Yousif's father and his eight-year-old brother, also the wife of his uncle, who was pregnant, and another uncle. The house is completely destroyed, everything they had is gone. Yousif got shot in his leg. He suffered multiple fractures. First we brought him to a hospital in Baghdad, but even there we did not feel safe. So we came here in a private car. He had to undergo surgery. He will get well and can continue his life, his studies. But we will never go back to Baghdad. Yousif's father was a brilliant man, he was an engineer. I told the boy that his father was still alive, but he answered: 'Don't lie to me, Uncle, I saw him lying there. I know he is dead.' He saw everything happen before his eyes. His little brother's body was full of bullets. They shot him with the machine gun. Yousif's mother is in Kirkuk now, since the attack she is having mental problems. She had suffered from rheumatism for a long time and now she cannot move at all. For the moment she does not get any medical care or counselling. Maybe we can bring her here next week. We are very thankful to this hospital and to the doctors who are helping us. The care here is very good.

Please, let the world know what is happening to us!" [12]

In the aftermath of war, rebuilding communities takes time; undoing the damage done to the land takes even longer. During the Vietnam War, American troops sprayed the defoliant, Agent Orange, over jungle areas and agricultural lands. Twenty-five years later, those areas are still contaminated, unable to grow food.

Two-thirds of Kuwait's underground aquifers, a major source of drinking water, are still polluted by oil spilled during the First Gulf War. NATO bombing campaigns in Kosovo targeted chemical plants and oil refineries. The result of one bombing raid in the city of Pancevo was that black rain fell on the city, releasing carcinogenic chemicals like dioxin in concentrations many thousands of times higher than recognized safety levels. The rains polluted the soil and poisoned crops - and those who ate them.[13]

*image - Killing field skulls, where almost 9,000 victims of the Pol Pot Khmer Rouge rested buried in mass graves. Many included women and children.

A third of the world's population is at war.

Chapter 7

STATELESSNESS

intro

Where are you from? What is your nationality? These are pretty common questions. Imagine not being able to give a straight answer. Imagine a life where no country will claim you as its own. This is a situation called Statelessness.

"No one shall be arbitrarily deprived of his nationality, nor denied the right to change his nationality."

- 1948 UN Declaration of Human Rights

Follow this process. A young expectant mother flees her war torn homeland due to economic and political exile. Two weeks after arriving in her new home country, her child is born. That child is not given a birth registration of any sort. That child, as far as the rest of the world is concerned, does not exist. The worst is yet to come as this little boy will not have the ability to go to school to get a proper education. No education and no birth certificate mean no real job opportunities. Some realistic options are bonded labour or crime. After a long life of manual labour and the frustration of not having a real identity, the final slap in the face is dealt; no death certificate, no real burial plot, no lasting proof of existence.

In the year 2000, the births of 4 out of every 10 children were not registered. These children will have no official existence or recognition of nationality. [1]

Photo: Augusto Rosales

147

Photo: Augusto Rosales

148

"My only crime is that I am not a citizen of any country."

Tom Chu is a 28-year-old Chinese man from Sri Lanka now studying abroad. "I am treated with suspicion at the immigration checkpoints no matter where I go, all due to my statelessness." Tom told Refugees International, "I was under the impression the UN passed an international law, Convention on the Reduction of Statelessness, requiring nations governed by international law to abide by this and provide citizenship to those who are stateless.

I suppose Sri Lanka either doesn't comply or the Constitution somehow supersedes such laws." [2]

Nationality is a legal bond between a State and an individual, and statelessness refers to the condition of an individual who is not considered as a national by any State under its domestic law. Although stateless people may sometimes also be refugees, the two categories are distinct. [3]

Statelessness is a massive problem that affects an estimated 15 million people in at least 60 developed and developing countries. Statelessness also has a terrible impact on the lives of individuals. Possession of nationality is essential for full participation in society and a prerequisite for the enjoyment of the full range of human rights. While human rights are generally to be enjoyed by everyone, rights such as the right to vote and the unrestricted right to enter and reside in a State may be limited to nationals. Of even greater concern is that many more rights of stateless persons are violated in practice: they may be detained for the sole reason that they are stateless, denied access to education and health services, or blocked from obtaining employment. [4]

"Everyone has the right to a nationality."

An ambitious 2003 global survey aimed for the first time to construct a comprehensive picture of statelessness. It identified current weaknesses in the system, underlined both the concerns and specific needs of affected states and will help the United Nations Refugee Agency develop a future blueprint to fulfill its role more effectively. Fewer than half of the responding governments, for instance, know the precise magnitude of the problem in their countries. Only around half have procedures to identify individuals who may actually be stateless, even though the same countries may have mechanisms to process refugee claimants. [5]

Photo: Stephanie Hunter

Kamal is one of the few Bidoon, (an Arabic term meaning "without nationality"), willing to talk about what it is like to be stateless in the United Arab Emirates. "What have we done to be treated like animals?" he asks. We can't get jobs and can't move. We are like a boat without a port." The struggles of the Bidoon are not limited to employment and travel. "Access to education is also a problem," Kamal says. "I didn't finish high school or go to college." Bidoon can seek health care at private hospitals, but not government ones. In Kamal's case, not being able to travel outside the UAE for specialized medical services meant that a treatable condition became a permanent disability. While some Bidoon are able to find work as drivers or mechanics, others survive by begging, an illegal activity in the UAE. Kamal says his sisters have married local men. Fifteen years from now they will be able to claim Emerati citizenship for themselves. "They have solved their problem," Kamal claims, "and their children have local nationality." [6]

Photo: Stephanie Hunter

154

In the Mirpur area of Dhaka, twenty-two-year-old Han spends his days in a small two-floor wooden structure completely filled by two huge looms and a set of narrow steps leading upstairs. Sitting for long hours at the machine is not physically difficult for him because he has worked like this since he was age ten. He can produce about three saris in a nine or ten hour work day, with a break every three hours. A six-meter garment made by two people is sold for about 300 Taka, approximately $5.00. Most of this earning is used to rent the equipment from a local Bangladeshi owner, and the rest Han uses to help support his parents and siblings. Han acknowledges that the camp where he lives needs education and a technical institution, but he says that what Biharis really need is a solution. "We are not citizens of Bangladesh or Pakistan. It's like being in a 'hanging position." [7]

Katrina says the current situation for "undetermined citizens" or gray passport holders "is all about politics." She says she is going to get a Russian passport. "My father came from the Ukraine, and my husband's family from Kazakhstan. He worked in a coal mine in Siberia for some 25-30 years." Katrina worked in a Russian school in Oru for almost as long and continues to help out part-time. The number of students at the school has now dropped from 400 to 200. Katrina gets a small pension for her work, over half of which goes to cover her rent. "Our situation is not good, but it could be worse," she says. There is little work for residents in a part of the country where unemployment hovers near 20 percent. Utilities, such as hot water, used to be provided free of charge, but recently the policy changed and now those who refuse to pay or cannot afford it, especially the elderly, go without. [8]

Adella and her two sons, aged 7 and 9, were brought to Sojourn House by a police officer late one night. She had been found wandering and crying in Toronto's Pearson International Airport. She spoke no English.

The next day, a Sojourn House counsellor met with her and discovered that Adella was also nine months pregnant. She had been taken from Afghanistan to a refugee camp at the Pakistani border by her brother when her husband disappeared. It is believed that he was abducted by the Taliban. In the rush and confusion to leave, fearing for her safety and the safety of her children, Adella became separated from her eldest son. He is 10 years old and she prays that he is with a neighbour in their village.

Her brother used his life savings to pay an agent to send Adella and her children to Canada where as a woman without a husband she would be safe, and her children would have a future.

Photo: Stephanie Hunter

I only know her first name: Danica. She was 18 months old, abandoned; a child of Haitian descent, whose parents had no citizenship, and were living in Dominican Republic. She was stateless, and no one knew she existed.

I only heard her cry once, and had never seen her give any response to anyone. My friends, Phil and Donna, had found her in a house where she had been left alone for up to 8 hours a day because her mother had abandoned her while her father was working in another part of the country. He had left people to watch over her, but he was nowhere to be found.

Absolute, as an organization, had decided that we would adopt her and commit to her medical and personal care. She was unable to walk or talk, and was very sick from a urinary tract infection that had been left untreated for weeks or even perhaps months. We had taken pictures of her and
were all excited to meet the family that was going to be taking care of her when she got out of the hospital.

Danica never made it out of the hospital. Danica had slipped into eternity, holding the hand of a stranger who had volunteered to stay up with her on her last night... another little nameless child, another victim of statelessness, caught in the vice-grip of poverty and lack of education. Danica is one of 30,000 children that died that day; all of them from totally preventable diseases, all of them just as valuable as our own children.

We couldn't bear the thought of no one being there to celebrate her life, so we gave her a proper funeral and burial. No one could find her family, so at 4:30 in the afternoon, twelve random Canadians, one translator and four Haitians from her village came out to celebrate her life. We could not celebrate her first steps, or her smile, or even the sound of her laughter, because we had never had the privilege of experiencing any of those things with her. We only knew of her struggle, her pain, and her abandonment. Instead, we came to celebrate her young life and to commit to something bigger than all of us: we will somehow, in some way, fight this evil predator called poverty. It is ruthless and cruel, it leaves a wake of destruction in it's path, but it can be confronted. I believe that we can do it. I really do.

Today, as I joined with my friends in putting flowers on Danica's tiny little grave, I made yet another resolution in my heart: her life will have counted for something and her story will be told.

Danica, I will tell your story. I will be your voice. I will fight for those who can't fight on their own. I will draw on the strength of my faith and resolve to be a strength wherever I can. I will choose, for your sake and the sake of so many more like you, to see the solution and not let the problem swallow me up.

Danica, your life has spoken to me, and your name will live on. Thank you for coming into my life and for renewing the passion to fight for many more like you...
I hardly knew you, but I love you.

Sleep well, little girl...

- Christal Earle - Co-Founder of
  Absolute Leadership Development

Photo: Augusto Rosales

I had no husband left, no children, no friends, no roof over my head, no past in short. I never imagined that when I left Rwanda, I would feel abruptly and profoundly torn apart.

Especially as the bodies of my husband and children lay in common graves, in this country which never wanted us. As far as I was concerned, I had nothing left to do on that soil, which swallowed up my family in an ocean of torture, humiliation, suffering unmatched - perpetrated by our brothers the Rwandans. I thought myself disgusted with my own country.

I knew very little of the Europe I felt myself drifting towards. Only its winter had stuck in my mind. There were no elegant women because of the coats, no birds singing to me in the morning to herald the day ahead, no flowers opening to smile at me, no life! Still, I no longer had a choice.

That was the continent that would perhaps accept me. Where I would have the right to live simply like a human being. A human being at the very bottom of the ladder: a refugee.

No, I thought, I cannot be a refugee. I will be a tourist who will sleep soundly, without fear of a machete descending on my neck. Without seeing every morning the criminal people who I love, who have just betrayed me. I will be back in two months.

Farewell to family.

This decision gave me goosebumps! Three children. Abandoning my family, my past, this life of 100 years in 100 days as if I were abandoning myself. I got up and went to see my children. Or rather their common grave, there down below behind Gaspard's house, the man who led them to be killed. Sitting on the grave, I started talking to them.

My dear children, forgive me for abandoning you. Forgive me for not being able to lead you to adulthood. Forgive me for letting you die so young. Forgive me for not having the courage to fend off with another machete the machetes that killed you. Forgive me for having been an unfit mother. I abandon you. I am going off to live in a country which knows virtually nothing of your ordeal. I am off to smile to people who may be partly responsible for your death.

I am off to look for the protection of those who were unable or unwilling to protect you. I am a cowardly mother, even more cowardly than your assassins. [10]

- Yolande Mukagasana, Author and Human Rights Campaigner

Photo: Augusto Rosales

162

Because of the poverty and political situations in Haiti, many Haitians immigrate illegally to Dominican Republic - immigrating usually means walking hundreds of miles over the mountains, or saving up enough money to pay someone to smuggle them across the border. But, once they're in DR, they have no legal status, no access to government health care or education, and because of the racism that exists between Dominicans and Haitians, the only jobs that they can usually get are low wage labour... or if they can't get that... the garbage dumps.

There was one little boy in the garbage dump this summer that changed my life. His name was Roberto. My friends and I found Roberto rummaging through a pile of garbage, away from the rest of the group. Through Spanish and some broken French he was able to communicate to us that he was looking for aluminum cans. The four of us started to help him search for them, in mounds of garbage under sweltering heat. After 20 minutes, I'd found two myself, and the rest of them had found five or six. Roberto gave us each a huge smile every time we put a can in his sack... and I asked him how much money he'd get once it was full. He said it was 4 pesos, which is around 12 cents Canadian. We tried to find as many cans as we could after that. I wanted to give him all the pesos I had with me, but I knew that would have taken away the dignity of his work. I also knew that returning to help his community, and showing him that some 'gringos' from across the world cared about him, was much more valuable than throwing some money at his immediate situation.

Roberto deserves to live in a country where he's a legal citizen who can go to school instead of working in a garbage dump. He deserves to have access to health care and proper nutrition. He deserves to grow up and get married in a recognized ceremony, and to someday pass these same rights on to his own children.

In short, Roberto deserves everything that you and I take for granted. But, because he's a refugee, Roberto will still be there, sweating in that garbage dump, until someone cares enough to do something about it.

- Cindy Stover - Absolute Leadership Development

Is not the existence of even
one single stateless person enough cause
for alarm throughout the world?

Chapter 8

DISEASES

intro

One life... one dollar!

Not a bad deal. If you were told that you could save a child's life for a dollar, you would do it in a heartbeat. The senseless reality is that millions of children in developing nations are dying because they cannot afford, or cannot access, an immunization that only costs one dollar.

When hundreds of thousands of people die in a hurricane or tsunami, the world seems to stand still. It seems so unfair that 'mother nature' would deal those cards to innocent, unsuspecting people. The element of surprise, combined with the fact that nothing could have prevented it, seems to create an eerie sense of awe. What, then, do we feel when more people die as a result of something that is completely preventable?

The only word to describe this is Injustice.

Have you ever had diarrhea? So have 300,000 poor children, but to them, it was fatal. Almost 11 million children under the age 5 died in 2000, mostly from preventable diseases.

Stop, read that again. Almost 11 million under the age of 5 died in 2000, mostly from preventable diseases. The Boeing 747-100SR airplane seats 550 people. It is like stacking a 747-100SR full of kids and then downing it into the ocean, every 24 minutes, every hour, every day, every week of the year. Have a nice sleep tonight.

How do we know that this situation is not getting any better? Because 97 percent of the world's population growth takes place in the developing world. This is true despite the sad fact that the infant mortality rate per 1000 births is 7 in northern Europe, 51 in South America, and 108 in Eastern Africa. [1]

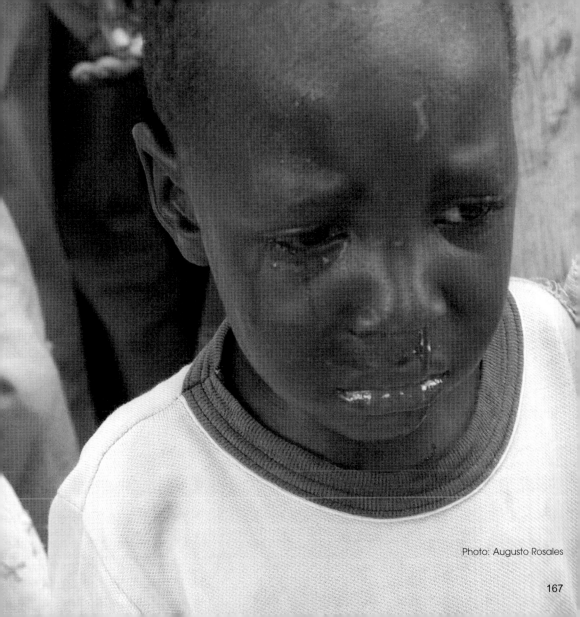

Photo: Augusto Rosales

There are 2.1 billion children in the world, accounting for 36% of the world's population. Some 132 million children are born each year. One of every 12 children dies before they reach five, mostly from preventable causes. [2]

Photo: Heather Bourque

Nazia and her brother are twins. Born in Karachi, Pakistan, both children have always been similar, growing up together, playing, laughing and crying together - until the day Nazia was diagnosed with polio.

Nazia and her brother are now two years old, but unlike her brother, Nazia can no longer walk.

While both children were born healthy, neither of them were given routine immunization to protect them against preventable diseases. The family never took the twins to a medical facility after birth, and the outreach vaccination teams missed their home.

It is a sad fact that when Nazia sees her twin brother get up and walk around, she tries to do the same but she can't. Nazia cries as she crawls across the floor, while her brother runs in front, not even looking back at Nazia to see her left behind. How Nazia will have to walk through her journey of life is of a huge concern for her parents.

Polio is the only vaccine preventable disease, after smallpox, that can be eradicated, and currently, most of the world is polio-free. There are only four countries in the world that are still polio endemic: Pakistan, Afghanistan, India and Nigeria. Pakistan has the chance to be the next polio-free country, but only if all children under five are given polio drops in every campaign - two drops of polio vaccine, every child, every time. [3]

The four most common childhood illnesses are diarrhea, acute respiratory illness, malaria and measles.

Each of these illnesses is both preventable and treatable. Yet, again, poverty interferes in parents' ability to access immunizations and medicines. Chronic undernourishment on top of insufficient treatment greatly increases a child's risk of death. [4]

Immunization

The so-called childhood diseases of measles, pertussis (whooping cough), tetanus, polio, and diphtheria are responsible for a little under a million deaths per year. Of these diseases, measles takes the greatest toll. All of these diseases are preventable through inexpensive vaccines. Typically a child will receive one vaccine for measles and one vaccine for the other three diseases combined.

Very recently, there has been great success with measles vaccinations. Between 2001 and 2005, the Measles Initiative, an international partnership backed by a number of organizations and individuals, vaccinated some 200 million children in poor countries. This cut the number of measles deaths by more than half.

At a cost of less than $1 per measles vaccination, this program shows how a relatively small amount of funding can make a huge difference in lives saved. There is no reason that this program cannot be extended to vaccinate all of the children who need it, provided enough funding is available. [5]

Respiratory Diseases

Pneumonia and other acute respiratory infections kill approximately two million children every year, making it the leading cause of death of children under five years of age. [6]

Since pneumonia is primarily caused by bacteria, the person can usually be treated with inexpensive antibiotics. If treated, pneumonia usually is not fatal.

The problem is that in very poor villages and communities there are often no doctors or health centres for treatment. A fairly recent innovation has been to train one person in each village or community to provide rudimentary health care, including dispensing common antibiotics. This common-sense solution has worked very well in many of the poorest areas of Africa, Asia, and South America. [7]

Photo: Augusto Rosales

Diarrheal disease kills 1.8 million children every year, primarily by causing severe dehydration that can quickly result in organ failure in young children. [8]

Strong, healthy people can recover from diarrhea in a few hours or days at most. However, individuals weakened by malnutrition or sickness often cannot recover and start losing large amounts of fluids and salts. Without treatment, this may continue until they actually die of dehydration. Children become dehydrated faster than adults.

The treatment for diarrhea is surprisingly simple. Called Oral Rehydration Therapy (ORT), it is a mixture of water, salt, and sugar that replenishes the lost fluids in the body. This basic treatment has helped reduce diarrheal deaths by about two-thirds in the last 25 years. It is perhaps the height of human tragedy that still so many parents must watch a son or daughter die of diarrhea when the cure is so simple and so inexpensive. [9]

Tuberculosis

In the entire history of humankind, it is believed that tuberculosis has killed more people than any other disease. (In shorter periods of time, the epidemics of the Bubonic Plague 'Black Death', and AIDS have killed more). [10]

Tuberculosis (TB) killed approximately 550,000 people in Africa last year. These global pandemics disproportionately affect the poorest of the poor. [11]

Tuberculosis is highly contagious and spreads through the air from coughing. If not treated, a person with TB infects an average of 10 to 15 new people each year. Once thought to be under control, tuberculosis still kills well over 1.5 million people each year, a figure that is now increasing slightly each year.

In 1995 the World Health Organization launched a multi-pronged tuberculosis program called DOTS (Directly Observed Therapy). Since then it has successfully treated more than 22 million tuberculosis patients. Funding is needed so that this effective program can expand to reach all the people who need it. [12]

Photo: Augusto Rosales

Malaria

Malaria is a long-lasting blood disease that is often fatal if left untreated. Once in the bloodstream, the parasite matures and multiplies and can destroy thousands of red blood cells in a few hours. Children, with their small bodies and immature immune systems, are particularly vulnerable to severe illness and death. In Africa, Malaria is the largest single cause of death among children under the age of five - killing one child every 30 seconds, more than 750,000 per year. Without concerted actions, the death rate is expected to double in the next 20 years.

Worldwide, between 350 and 500 million people are infected with Malaria annually,[13] over a million people die from malaria each year and many millions more are seriously weakened by it. One bite from an infected mosquito can mean weeks of fever and exhaustion, preventing children from going to school and adults from working to provide for their families. Close to 90% of malaria cases occur in Africa.

Although malaria is treatable with anti-malarial drugs, these are often not available in the poorest areas.[14] Additionally, many children who survive are left with persistent anaemia, lifelong brain damage or paralysis. Malaria in pregnant women can lead to low birth weight, anaemia and a greater risk of neonatal death to their babies.

Since Malaria carrying mosquitoes bite at night while families are sleeping, insecticide-treated bed nets (mosquito nets) are the most effective and inexpensive way to prevent transmission of Malaria. Not only do they provide a physical barrier to mosquitoes, reducing the chances of being bitten, the bed nets are treated with insecticide so the mosquitoes are killed on contact. The use of these nets has been shown to reduce mortality in children under the age of five from all causes by up to 25 per cent.

Besides saving lives, bed nets are an excellent investment, as Malaria has reduced economic growth in African countries by as much as 1.3 per cent per year and is responsible for more than US$14-billion annually in healthcare costs and lost productivity. In Africa, Malaria accounts for 40 per cent of public health expenditures.[15]

177

90% of worldwide Malaria cases occur in Sub-Saharan Africa, including Liberia and Rwanda, where just about every child has first hand experience with the dreaded disease. The countries' tropical rain forests and wetlands provide the perfect breeding grounds for mosquitoes that carry the Malaria parasite.

In Liberia

- 235 out of 1,000 kids under the age of 5 die each year.
- 32% of these children die from Malaria.

In Rwanda

- 152 out of 1,000 kids under the age of 5 die each year.
- 42% of these children die from Malaria. [16]

More people die every single month in Africa from AIDS and malaria alone than died in the entirety of the 2004 Asia-Pacific tsunami. [17]

"What can I do to prevent malaria?" asks Bizunesh, lying on a thin mattress on the floor at an Ethiopian Hospital with a quinine drip attached to her arm. Next to her lay one of her daughters, a pink scarf wrapped around her head to keep the warmth in and minimize the bounding headaches the malaria causes. "My husband has died. I have four children. What can a wife and children do alone?" Her voice gets more agitated as tears well in her eyes and she begins to cry. All her children are suffering from malaria during this current epidemic.

Mattresses line the corridors. Makeshift beds are made on the wooden benches and people share whatever space they can find. The wards are all full. It is the rainy season, and already hundreds of people have been diagnosed with the disease and been hospitalized. With chloroquine drug resistance high, the large majority needs to be treated with quinine, and put on drips, stretching already overburdened services and exhausted staff.

Bizunesh simply can not afford to be sick. Raising her four children alone she is dependent on trading in small grocery items and growing food on her small plot of land. Lying in hospital, she hopes to be able to go home in a day or two, but she is worried how she will manage while all the children are still weak from the disease. Her small savings have vanished and she no longer knows how she will continue to feed them, let alone keep them healthy. [18]

Vitamin Deficiencies

- 2 million children may die unnecessarily each year because they lack vitamin A, Zinc, or other nutrients.
- 19 million infants are born with impaired mental capacity every year due to iodine deficiency.
- 100,000 babies are born each year with preventable physical defects
- Iron deficiency undermines the health and energy of 40 percent of women in the developing world. Severe anemia kills more than 60,000 women each year, especially during childbirth.
- Vitamin and mineral deficiencies account for 10 percent of the global health burden. [19]

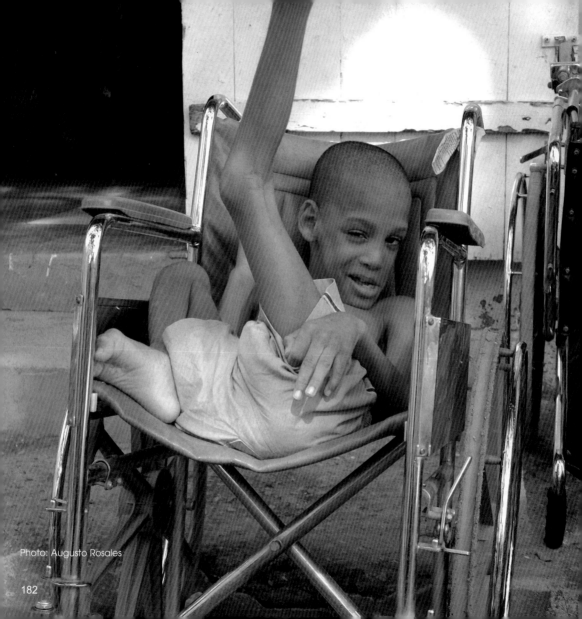

Photo: Augusto Rosales

Every year, our grade seven students line up for a long needle from the health nurse which immunizes them from a laundry list of diseases. Every day, 6,000 kids in a very different part of the world die because they don't have the opportunity to wait in those lines. [20]

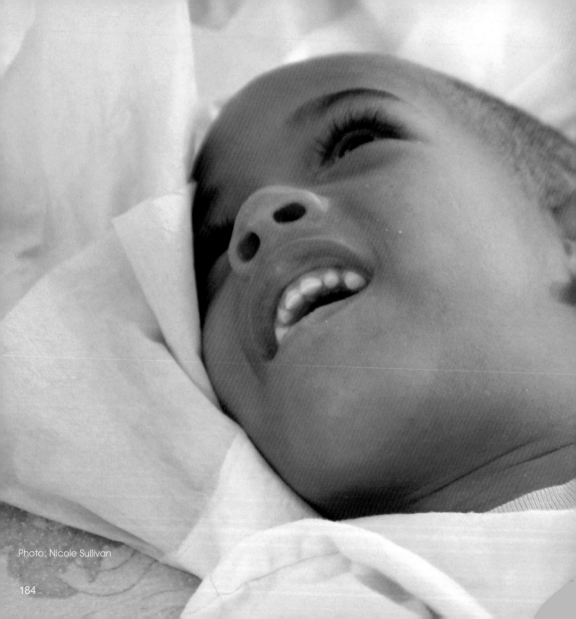

Photo: Nicole Sullivan

184

It's just after dawn and Riniyati is getting her 11-month-old baby girl Tresia ready for the day. She softly tells Tresia that today is special. Today she will go to the village longhouse to be immunized. Tresia is one of the 14 million children who are being immunized in Indonesia this year. Some live in cities and towns across this vast archipelago. But many, like Riniyati and Tresia, live in remote areas where getting the lifesaving vaccine is not an easy task.

About an hour away, a UNICEF Project Officer, Dr. Wibowo, is making his way up the mountain by motorcycle carrying measles and polio vaccines, as well as immunity-boosting vitamin A supplements.

The vaccines have travelled far. From the factory in West Java they were flown to the provincial capital, where they were sent by road to district health offices - and then carried by boat and by hand to this remote outpost.

"It is vital that we reach every child," says Dr. Wibowo. "There is also a need to inform parents about the importance of immunization, and what could happen if they do not bring their children to health clinics or the temporary immunization posts like the ones here in this village." [21]

Mare Alehegn lays back nervously on the metal operating table, her heart visibly pounding beneath her sackcloth dress, and clenched her fists as the paramedic sliced into her eyelid. Repeated infections had scarred the undersides of her eyelids, causing them to contract and forcing her lashes in on her eyes. For years, each blink felt like thorns raking her eyeballs. She had plucked the hairs with crude tweezers, but the stubble grew back sharper still.

The scratching, for Mrs. Alehegn, 42, and millions worldwide, gradually clouds the eyeball, dimming vision and, if left untreated, eventually leads to a life shrouded in darkness. This is late-stage trachoma, a neglected disease of neglected people, and a preventable one, but for a lack of the modest resources that could defeat it. This operation, which promised to lift the lashes off Mrs. Alehegn's lacerated eyes, is a 15-minute procedure so simple that a health worker with a few weeks of training can do it. The materials cost about $10.

The operation, performed last year, would not only deliver Mrs. Alehegn from disabling pain and stop the damage to her corneas, but it also would hold out hope of a new life for her daughter, Enatnesh, who waited vigilantly outside the operating room door at the free surgery camp here.

Mrs. Alehegn's husband left her years ago when the disease rendered her unable to do a wife's work. At 6, Enatnesh was forced to choose between a father who could support her, or a lifetime of hard labor to help a mother who had no one else to turn to.

"I chose my mother," said the frail, pigtailed slip of a girl, so ill fed that she looked closer to 10 than her current age, 16. "If I hadn't gone with her, she would have died. No one was there to even give her a glass of water."

Their tale is common among trachoma sufferers. Trachoma's blinding damage builds over decades of repeated infections that begin in babies. The infections are spread from person to person, or by hungry flies that feed from seeping eyes. For many women, the pain and eventual blindness ensure a life of deepening destitution and dependency. They become a burden on daughters and granddaughters, making trachoma a generational scourge among women and girls who are often already the most vulnerable of the poor.

The World Health Organization estimates that 70 million people are infected with trachoma. Five million suffer from its late stages. And two million are blind because of it. [22]

The fundamental difference between now and five decades ago is that we have the knowledge and proven cost-effective technologies to prevent and treat these childhood threats - including pneumonia, diarrheal disease, malaria and measles - yet these are still the leading causes of preventable death for the world's children.

- Nigel Fisher, President and CEO of UNICEF Canada. [23]

What we're seeing, when we go in to do disaster relief, is that more and more frequently, the disaster is the tip of the iceberg. The real problem is that the basic health of that community has been going steadily down over the last decade.

- Peter Walker, Director of Disaster Policy for the International federation of the Red Cross. [24]

189

2 million children die of preventable diseases each year because they have not been immunized.

Chapter 9

THIRST

intro

Recently, I was sitting with some friends in their home getting ready to do a presentation to a small peer group that they were trying to motivate in the area of global issues. As the evening progressed and the snacks came out, their extremely large chocolate lab, Charlie, began frantically roaming through the house in hope of finding a cracker that had fallen to the floor.

When the discussion got started, I discovered that the group was preparing to travel to Mexico in two weeks to do humanitarian work. We began talking about the injustice in the world and Wendy, Charlie's owner, shared a brilliant insight.

"Today, as I was feeding Charlie, I decided that I would top up his water bowl. When the bowl was full, I suddenly realized that there was a hair in the water. Without giving it a second thought, I dumped out the water and refilled it with a clean bowl. At that moment the thought came to me that a large part of the world contains people that would give anything for the water that I just poured down the drain. I, however, felt that my dog deserved water that did not contain a hair. I felt sick to my stomach with what had transpired."

The fact is that we can take so many things for granted. In the West we consider clean water a right while much of the world is forced to consider it a privilege.

Photo: Nicole Sullivan

193

Would you deny for others what you demand for yourself?

You speak of signs and wonders, but I need something other.
I would believe if I was able, but I'm waiting on the crumbs from your table.

Where you live should not decide, whether you live or whether you die.
Three to a bed, sister and she said, dignity passed us by.

Crumbs From Your Table - U2

Photo: Stephanie Hunter

195

30,000 people were killed in armed conflicts in 2000...
as many people die each and every month because of
contaminated water or lack of adequate sanitation.[1]

Growing up in a village in Angola, Fatima had to spend up to four hours every day collecting water from the river. It was a dangerous trek. One year, seven of Fatima's friends were attacked by crocodiles.

But the girls carried a much bigger danger back with them to the village. The water was polluted and spread disease. As a result, when Fatima herself was not sick, she had to spend many hours each week caring for sick brothers and sisters, and when she grew older, for her own sick children.

In 1999, Fatima's first child died after a repeated illness with diarrhea. "Isabel was always sick, she could just never get strong," says Fatima, hugging her second child, 13-month-old Fernando. "By the time Isabel was Fernando's age she had been sick a dozen times. But, this boy has never once had diarrhea. Not once."

In 2000 the Angolan Government and UNICEF teamed up to lay a pipeline from the river to the community where Fatima lived. Latrines, washbasins, taps and showers were then built, together with a filtering system to ensure every drop of water was drinkable. As a result, diarrhea rates dropped almost to zero, child deaths plummeted, and many girls (who no longer had to spend hours every day carrying water) entered school for the first time. A community water and sanitation committee now maintains the system and teaches hygiene to the rest of the community.

Unfortunately, Fatima's village remains the exception rather than the rule in Angola. Almost three decades of war have left millions of people without clean water or basic sanitation. A huge task remains: drilling boreholes across the country, constructing major pipelines, establishing a national sanitation education campaign, and providing water to schools. [2]

Photo: Augusto Rosales

Photo: Stephanie Hunter

Clean water is an inviolable right, not a privilege.

- Carol Bellamy, Former Executive Director, UNICEF

Two buckets of safe water a day - 20 litres - is the bare minimum a child needs to live. This is enough for drinking and eating, washing and basic sanitation. But some 4000 children die every day, because they simply don't have access to an adequate supply of clean water. In many communities, families are forced by poverty and scarcity to rely on unsafe sources of water like ponds, open wells or street vendors. Many have to walk miles each day to collect enough water to drink, cook and wash. [3]

Water is fundamental to human life, health and dignity. But, despite great efforts in many countries, over one billion people worldwide struggle daily without the bare minimum of safe water they need to survive. And gains in bringing safe water to families are being washed away by the appalling lack of progress on basic sanitation. One third of the world's population - 2.6 billion people - are without access to a basic latrine. [4]

Lam and Quyen are both shorter than they should be for their eight years. The reason is simple: poor sanitation.

Lam and Quyen live in Minh Luong, in Vietnam. Both boys fell victim to intestinal parasitic infections ("worms") caused by unclean conditions. They are far from being alone: according to Government statistics, levels of such infections are as high as 97 per cent! These infections contribute to high levels of protein-energy malnutrition, which is what stunted Lam's and Quyen's growth.

But Lam and Quyen were lucky. It used to be common for children in Minh Luong to die of water-related diseases. "I gave birth to nine children," says Vit, who is now a grandmother in her 60s, "but only three survived. Six died from silly diseases like diarrhea or measles that today you can prevent with good hygiene, care and medicine."

Despite continued efforts by Government and international agencies, overall sanitation coverage in Vietnam remains low. Probably fewer than 30 per cent of rural households have access to a latrine that meets UNICEF's design standards, and even fewer know how to use latrines hygienically. [5]

In Sub-Saharan Africa, 43 percent of children drink unsafe water and one in five die before their fifth birthday. In South Asia, only 35 percent of children have access to even a basic latrine. [6]

A lack of clean water and basic sanitation is responsible for 1.6 million preventable child deaths each year. Millions more children suffer from waterborne illnesses, such as typhoid, worms and diarrhea. Repeated episodes of diarrhea leave millions more with a permanent legacy of malnourishment and ill-health. With their physical and intellectual development eroded, many will find school and learning impossible. [7]

Photo: Augusto Rosales

Over half of all schools worldwide lack adequate water and sanitation facilities, which is harmful to both childrens' health and their education. The situation is particularly critical for girls, who make up most of the 115 million children currently out of school. Many are denied their rightful place in the classroom by lack of access to separate and decent toilets at school, or else the daily chore of walking miles to collect water for the family. [8]

For many poor children, school is the only opportunity they have to discover the critical links between good hygiene and health. Trained teachers can help children learn health-promoting skills such as hand-washing before eating or safe waste disposal. Good hygiene education transforms children into health educators for their families, passing on vital information and skills which can reduce household vulnerability to deadly waterborne diseases. Hand-washing alone can reduce deadly diarrheal diseases by at least 40 per cent. [9]

In a ward of the children's hospital in Iraq, nine-month-old Ibrahim is in a deep sleep. His mother, Wedad, sits beside him fanning his face. "He is so weak and dry," Wedad says. "He had 15 bouts of diarrhea last month. I've done everything I can to help him, but he is still ill."

Life is tough for the whole family. Ibrahim's father has no regular work and it is difficult to get enough food. But the biggest problem is the shortage of clean drinking water.

Every second day, Wedad buys five litres of water from a private water tankering company.

"I keep it for the children to drink but it's never enough," she says. "The water they bathe in and which I use to prepare food comes direct from the tap. It tastes bad and has a strange colour, but what can you do?"

Years of under-investment, more than 12 years of sanctions and two wars had left Iraq's water system in a bad state of repair. After the most recent conflict, vital equipment was looted from many pumping stations and water-treatment plants. When Ibrahim's story was filed by UNICEF in 2003, UNICEF was providing 14.6 million litres of water daily to over 825,000 people. Urgent work continues to distribute emergency water supplies, repair water and sewage systems, and supply new equipment. [10]

Children forced to drink unsafe water and live in unsanitary conditions cannot thrive. But when their lives are protected, their families are strengthened and their own children are likely to be born with better prospects. It's the surest, shortest, smartest route to a more hopeful future.

> - Carol Bellamy, Former Executive Director, UNICEF

My school is 4 kilometers away from my residence. The school has no water supply and latrine facilities. Students go to the nearby bushes to ease themselves. My fellow students and I, including the whole community, drink water from the river, which is polluted. We don't only drink it, but we also use it for washing clothes and cooking food. To get water from where we live we have to walk 5 to 6 kilometers. In order not to waste water extravagantly, we have to minimize our water usage. So we do not even drink water whenever we need it in order not to walk those miles again, let alone using it for personal hygiene.

The water we use for our different needs is not safe and clean. There are lots of bacteria in it. Some people swim in it or wash cars in it. People even defecate beside the river, and whenever there is rain it washes it down to the river, polluting the water. This problem is not only in the town where I live, but in the rural areas too. Life in the rural areas is more difficult because they get their water from a river and they have to walk 10 to 15 kilometers. This water is not only drunk by people but also by animals, and because of that people get sick with lots of water-borne diseases. These water-borne diseases attack children, which is the major problem preventing children from attending school.

To help our families, we students have formed a school sanitation club. We learn basic hygiene skills, and pass them on to our friends and relations. So I would like to request international organizations to help us get clean drinking water, and to help us get latrines and clean water in our schools and communities. I am asking this in the name of our children, women and the whole community.

> - Ojulu, a Student from Ethiopia [11]

A lack of water is not just an inconvenience for women it actually enslaves them. Once you provide water and sanitation, it really liberates them and it really opens up a virtuous cycle of development: girls can go to school; they will become better mothers, better citizens and that leads to national development.

- Kul Gautam, Assistant Secretary-
General of the United Nations and
Deputy Executive Director, UNICEF

Today there are 400 million children worldwide without enough safe drinking water to live. This is wrong. This is killing our future. We call on you to act.

United, we call for action to support the participation of children in water, environment, sanitation and hygiene education, to meet the Millennium Development Goals.

We, the children of the world, are ready to work with you. Are you ready to work with us?

- The Children's Water Manifesto;
complied by Children from 29
countries participating in the
2nd Children's World Water
Forum, 2006

For us, thirst is annoying. For children at risk, it can be deadly.

Chapter 10

CORRUPTION

I find it very difficult to write about corruption.

The fact that innocent children suffer to fulfill someone's selfish desires and greed is bad enough in the cases of slavery and trafficking. This, however, goes to a new level when the abuser is an authority figure. When police, politicians and even world leaders, place their own selfish ambition over the needs of the people that they are serving, a supreme injustice has taken place.

This is a growing dilemma among aid workers, NGO's and advocates globally. There is never enough money to meet the needs but, more importantly, there is a lack of trust in governments and financial institutions to administrate the little money that there is. Even with unlimited resources, could we end world poverty? Do we have a way to guarantee that the help gets to the places where it is needed to most?

I was recently in Haiti delivering medical supplies for a mobile clinic. As we were approaching the city, a local guide told me endless stories of relief workers that were murdered by authorities for the supplies that they were carrying. Although I would have appreciated that information before I entered the country, I was impacted by the notion that relief workers often risked their own lives to extend help to those in need.

Corruption makes it difficult for the well intentioned to make a real difference.

It is poverty to decide that a child must die so that you may live as you wish.

- Mother Theresa

Photo: Augusto Rosales

215

Every country has terrorists.

Some are rebels, some are elected.

Some wear traditional religious garments,
some wear three piece suits.

Ugandans are all too acquainted with the concept of corruption. The Lord's Resistance Army, under the leadership of Joseph Kony, has terrorized the people of that country under the guise of 'Christianity' for years. Perverting the teachings of the Bible and the Ten Commandments, Kony has abducted an estimated 25,000 children. With a trail of murder and rape following him and his army, Kony personifies 'passion' gone wrong.

Jennifer and Susan, arms linked, backs straight, hair tightly shaved, hiked dusty trails without shoes, their feet swollen and callused. They walked with thousands of other children, all rushing away from the danger of nighttime rebel raids on their villages and toward the safety of the town centre to sleep. Tiny boys in tattered clothing, girls with chubby cheeks clutching ragged dolls, others with foam mattresses balanced on their heads, others with nothing at all, were walking.

Jennifer and Susan sang a marching song. "People in Gulu are suffering. Education is poor. Communication is poor. There are no more virgins in Gulu," the girls sang sweetly in English. "They were all raped. Hear us now: There are no more virgins in Gulu."

The children are called simply "the night commuters" or "night dwellers." About 15,000 young Ugandans trek every evening from more than 300 villages, some more than five miles away into the safety of Gulu, about 175 miles north of the capital, Kampala. [1]

Poverty is like punishment for a crime you didn't commit.

- Eli Khamarov

Photo: Augusto Rosales

220

In any country in the world, it is a heavy burden to be poor. But citizens of highly corrupt countries face challenges of a different magnitude. Despite some gains, corruption remains an enormous drain on resources that are sorely needed to feed, clothe and educate millions of human beings. The African Union has estimated the total annual cost of corruption to the continent at just under 150 billion US dollars, far outstripping global development assistance spending.

Poor countries face enormous challenges as they struggle to feed their people and ensure education for their children in an environment of severe deprivation. But corruption is not simply a problem of poor countries, as continuing corporate and government scandals show. And with the cross-border nature of corruption in poorer countries, rich and poor nations share the heavy responsibility of breaking the corruption cycle.

The world's richest countries tend to have powerful advantages: political stability, material wealth, mature freedom of information and regulatory regimes, and a relatively clean public sector. But there is an unseemly dark side: these countries are often complicit in driving corruption in poor nations, and in stymieing efforts to return funds stolen by corrupt officials.

Corruption becomes systematic, incorporated into daily business life, seen as a way of doing business, cynically cast as respect for local traditions by companies that would never behave similarly at home. Recent corporate corruption cases show that the phenomenon can persist despite a strong anti-corruption regime in countries, countries perceived as 'clean'.

But corruption isn't just brown envelopes, slipped under tables or passed in dark alleys. Too often it has meant wholesale theft of public resources by leaders and high-level public officials exploiting pliant or non-existent enforcement systems. Billions of dollars of this money, so desperately needed for basic services in the poorest countries, has quietly traversed borders and landed in bank accounts in financial centres in some of the wealthiest places on earth. In many cases, the recovery of these looted and laundered assets is hindered by bank secrecy. Progress has been made, but global financial centres still bear a heavy responsibility in repatriating this wrongfully acquired wealth. [2]

Photo: Heather Bauque

The world is very different now. For man holds in his mortal hands the power to abolish all forms of human poverty, and all forms of human life.

- John Fitzgerald Kennedy

I remember being in Malawi in 2002 at a roundtable discussion with the vice-president and a number of civil servants from the Ministry of Finance. They were complaining bitterly about the limits imposed by the International Monetary Fund on Malawi's public sector pay levels and hiring intentions.

It was surreal: here you had a country with huge human capacity problems that wanted desperately to retain its professionals in health and education, and increase their numbers, but the IMF wouldn't allow them to do so. We're talking about a sovereign government, fighting the worst plague in history, with but a handful of professionals: according to the minister of health, Malawi has one-third of the nurses it needs (four thousand instead of the necessary twelve thousand) and perhaps 10 percent of the doctors (three hundred rather than three thousand) for a population of twelve million. And they weren't being allowed - I repeat, this sovereign government wasn't being allowed - to hire more staff and pay better salaries, because it would breach the macroeconomic straitjacket.

What makes me nearly apoplectic - and I very much want to say this - is that the Bank and the Fund were fully told about their mistakes even as the mistakes were being made. It's so enraging that they refused to listen. They were so smug, so all-knowing, so incredibly arrogant, so wrong. They simply didn't respond to arguments which begged them to review the human consequences of their policies. The fact that poverty became increasingly entrenched, or that economies were not responding to the dogma as the dogma predicted, made no difference. It was a form of capitalist Stalinism. The credo was everything; the people were a laboratory. [3]

- Stephen Lewis, Former UN Special
Envoy for HIV/AIDS in Africa

Must we starve our children to pay our debts? That question has now been answered in practice. And the answer has been "Yes." In these three years, hundreds of thousands of the developing world's children have given their lives to pay their countries' debts, and many millions more are still paying the interest with their malnourished minds and bodies... the fact that so much of today's staggering debt was irresponsibly borrowed would matter less if the consequences of such folly were falling on its perpetrators. Yet now, when the party is over and the bills are coming in, it is the poor who are being asked to pay. Today, the heaviest burden of a decade of frenzied borrowing is falling not on the military or on those with foreign bank accounts or on those who conceived the years of waste, but on the poor who are having to do without necessities... on the women who do not have enough food to maintain their health, on the infants whose minds and bodies are not growing properly... and on the children who are being denied their only opportunity ever to go to school. In short, it is hardly too brutal an oversimplification to say that the rich got the loans and the poor got the debts. And when the impact becomes visible in rising death rates among children... then it is essential to strip away the niceties of economic parlance and say that what has happened is simply an outrage against a large section of humanity. The developing world's debt, both in the manner in which it was incurred and in the manner in which it is being 'adjusted to,' is an economic stain on the second half of the twentieth century. Allowing world economic problems to be taken out on the growing minds and bodies of young children is the antithesis of all civilized behaviour. Nothing can justify it. And it shames and diminishes us all.

- Julius Nyerere, former President of
Tanzania, in the UNICEF "State of
the World's Children" report of 1989.

227

The bottom line is that the excess of the West could alleviate the global hunger crisis if utilized appropriately.

When people in Ethiopia were starving in the mid 1980's, the North American grain market was booming. In fact, to save the stability of the wheat prices, many farmers were paid to 'ocean dump' their excess yield. Think this through for a moment: Other human beings are starving to death and our greed drives us to throw excess food away in an effort keep our future market strong.

North American journalist Paul Harvey commented on the relationship between people's religious beliefs and poverty. "There is no way that you and I are ever going to comprehend a society that feeds cows and starves babies," Harvey writes, speaking of the land of India and his understanding of the Hindu religion's sacred cows.

But one wonders which culture, India's or affluent Western nations, has the most "sacred cows." While our sacred cows are not part of recognizable religious traditions, American families feed their cattle 1,800 pounds of protein-rich grain in order to produce 250 pounds of meat for our dinner table. [4]

229

Esther came to the police station on a Friday to visit her husband Peter who had been arrested for an argument with a neighbour. Expecting his release, Esther returned to the station the following day to find her husband's body lying face-up in a pool of blood and the door to his cell lying broken beside him. Attempting to cover up the incident, the police commander told Esther that her husband had died from self-inflicted wounds by banging himself against the walls of the holding cell. An autopsy later revealed severe head and chest injuries, traumatic bruising and massive internal bleeding, likely caused by the police who held Peter in custody.

A local priest referred the family, which could not afford an advocate, to International Justice Mission staff who stood with Esther and her 12-year-old son, John. IJM investigated the case and presented conclusive intervention reports to local authorities proving the police were responsible for Peter's death. IJM continues to follow-up on the case to bring accountability to those who killed Peter. In December 2003, IJM staff visited Peter's grave with his mother, Esther and their son. The sunken plot was unmarked - its wooden marker stolen for firewood.

Peter's mother remarked that despite terrible circumstances they remain prayerful, even when thinking of the people who committed the crime against her son and perpetrated injustice against their family. "You must have a forgiving heart," she added. "To forgive even our enemies - to love our enemies." Esther encourages others to remain patient and asked for prayer "that this case may be resolved." [5]

Diamonds have helped fund devastating civil wars in Africa, destroying the lives of millions. Conflict diamonds are those sold in order to fund armed conflict and civil war. Profits from the trade in conflict diamonds, worth billions of dollars, were used by warlords and rebels to buy arms during the devastating wars in Angola, the Democratic Republic of Congo (DRC) and Sierra Leone. Wars that have cost an estimated 3.7 million lives. While the wars in Angola and Sierra Leone are now over, and fighting in the DRC has decreased, the problem of conflict diamonds hasn't gone away. Diamonds mined in rebel-held areas in Ivory Coast, a West African country in the midst of a volatile conflict, are reaching the international diamond market. Conflict diamonds from Liberia are also being smuggled into neighbouring countries and exported as part of the legitimate diamond trade. [6]

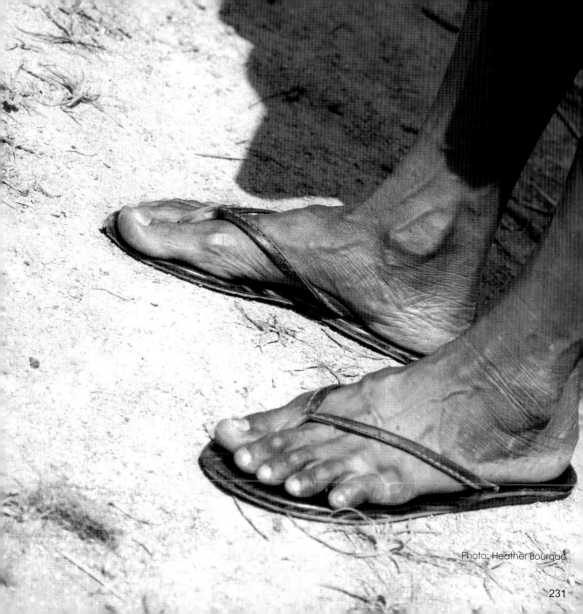

Photo: Stephanie Hunter

232

In April 2001, when Jusu Lahia was 15 years old, he was wounded by an exploding rocket-propelled grenade. A lieutenant in Sierra Leone's Revolutionary United Front (RUF), Lahia was picked off during a battle in one of the most remote corners of the planet. He was among thousands of victims of a war fought for control of one of the world's most precious commodities: a fortune in raw diamonds that have made their way from the deadly jungles of Sierra Leone onto the rings and necklaces of happy lovers the world over.

When Lahia sprawled to the earth - shards of hot metal ripped his body from face to groin, destroying his left eye - few who eventually wore the gems he fought over could even locate Sierra Leone. And fewer still could find the Parrot's Beak, a small wedge of land that juts between the borders of neighbouring Liberia and Guinea, directly into the line of fire between warring rebel factions in those countries. Rebel forces of all three nations were shooting it out with one another, as well as with the legitimate governments of all three countries and with an unknown number of local indigenous militias that were fighting for reasons of their own. The baffling and intense crossfire made the Parrot's Beak one of the deadliest 50-square-mile plots of land on the planet in 2001, and when Lahia went down in a hail of exploding shrapnel, he likely knew that he was far from the type of medical help that could save his life.

The RUF child soldier did not suffer alone. In the Parrot's Beak in mid-2001, some 50,000 refugees from Sierra Leone, Liberia, and Guinea were steadily dying from starvation, disease, and war wounds. The region was too hot for even the most daredevil humanitarian relief organizations.

Lahia was carried to a bare, fire-blackened hospital room in Kailahun, the RUF's stronghold in the Parrot's Beak, and dumped on a pile of hay that served as a bed. When I first saw him there, surrounded by chaos, heat, and filth, I found it hard to remember that the cause of all this suffering - thousands of doomed refugees, well-armed but illiterate and drugged combatants, fallen wounded like Lahia, and injured civilian children - was brutally simple: the greed for diamonds. Certainly, there was nothing nearly as lustrous or awe-inspiring as a diamond in the blood-stained room where Lahia was dying of a tetanus infection, next to another felled 15 year-old. Powerless to treat him, the RUF field medics had simply taped his wounds shut and left him wracked with sweats and shivers. [7]

We have laws in every country that say you can't abduct people, you can't kidnap, you can't force them into prostitution, you can't assault them - all kinds of laws that if you would enforce them, it would stop this kind of stuff. If you look at countries like Russia, which is one of the most corrupt countries, if you look at the situations that Ukraine and Romania find themselves in; or Moldova, which is one of the most impoverished countries on the planet - these countries just don't bother. And these are the countries from which the women are being trafficked. *This can be stopped!* The laws are there, but for some reason they're not being enforced. They're not being enforced, as far as I'm concerned, because of corruption, complicity and complacency.

It is a problem in Canada, where 2,000 to 3,000 of these young women are brought in every year. It's a problem in the United States, where 20,000 to 40,000 women are trafficked every year. It's a huge problem throughout the European Union, particularly in Germany, the Netherlands, even Great Britain, even Spain, Italy, Turkey, Greece. You find these women everywhere. You find them in Japan, in Hong Kong. You find them in the strangest of places, like Costa Rica and Dominican Republic.

There are all kinds of ways that people can get into North America: under student visas, temporary work orders, or tourism visas. You can get into Canada by taking a boat. A lot of these freighters come over, and in the back of them are girls and there are women, so when they park their little boats... in Vancouver or in Halifax or Montreal late at night, they're taken off, and they're *being exploited* here.

Wherever there seems to be a lonely guy looking for a woman, you'll find trafficked women. The police and government officials in every one of these countries know these women and girls are there, but don't do a damn thing about it. This is a Western problem that was created by the insatiable demand of the West. [8]

Photo: Stephanie Hunter

Photo: Augusto Rosales

Corruption has many faces and they are not all political. The following story is an example of how corrupt religious practices can lead desperate people to do desperate things.

Cape Town, South Africa, is reputed to be the most beautiful city in the world. However, the following report is from a part of town you won't see on your bus tour. (If you are squeamish, you may want to skip over this story.)

In the late 1990's, a high-ranking South African witch doctor made a public announcement that having sex with a virgin will cure HIV and AIDS. In a study in 2000, it was shown that 58 children were raped or victims of attempted rape every day. Over 15 percent of all South African rapes occur against children under the age of 11. That is about seven primary school-aged children each day. But some aren't even old enough for kindergarten. They haven't even learned to talk:

In 2001, a nine-month-old baby girl who survived a gang rape underwent a full hysterectomy and will require further surgery to repair intestinal damage. The baby was left unattended by her 16-year-old mother when six men allegedly raped her. The six men, aged between 22 and 66, appeared in court on charges of rape and indecent assault.

Later that year, a month-old baby girl was raped, allegedly by her uncles. A police spokesperson said the mother of the child had left the baby in the care of the men when she went to visit her mother-in-law. Upon her return, she found the baby crying and as she lifted her, she saw blood on her bottom. She then took the baby to a clinic where she was told the girl had been raped and sustained vaginal damage. [9]

It may seem hard to believe, but between 1970 and 2002, Africa acquired $294 billion of debt. Much of the debt was assumed by military dictators who profited beyond the dreams of avarice, and left for the people of their countries, the crushing burden of payment. Over the same period, it paid back $260 billion mostly in interest. And the end of it all, Africa continued to owe upwards of $230 billion in debt. Surely that is the definition of international economic obscenity. Here you have the poorest continent in the world paying off its debt, again and again, and forever being grotesquely in hock. [10]

Photo: Heather Bourque

239

The bribe money that buys a champagne
lifestyle for corrupt officials in the poorest nations
often originates in multinational companies
based in the world's richest countries.

Chapter 11

EDUCATION

intro

As I stood in the final debriefing meeting for one of our larger Hero Holiday® humanitarian trips recently, I was astounded by the words that I heard from our lead doctor for the project. In the presence of the group of students and adults, the doctor declared, "you will save more lives by building schools than you will ever save by building clinics." Those words still resonate in my heart. Providing an opportunity for education provides a greater opportunity for survival.

A little while ago I interviewed a gentleman in Dominican Republic who had helped us build a school in a poor village. I asked him what he thought about various countries in the Western World having a teen drop out rate as high as 20%. He asked me to repeat the question because he thought he had misunderstood me. I repeated the question and his face dropped. "You mean they are allowed to go to school and do not?"

Education may not be available to all, but it is the basic building block to a better life. A basic education gives an individual the ability to minimize the effects of other atrocities in their world.

The children of mothers who have a primary education are 50% more likely to reach the age of five. [1]

Our lives begin to end the moment we remain silent about things that matter.

- Martin Luther King, Jr

Illiteracy is the condition of being unable to read or write in any language - it almost sounds like a fatal disease, and it's spreading across the world's population. The most recent statistics estimate there to be nearly 800 million illiterate people in the world, 64 percent of which are women. These people are the most impoverished and marginalized in our society, but according to Article 26 of the Universal Declaration of Human Rights, education is a basic human right that everyone has. If education is a freedom of equality, why are there millions of illiterates in our global communities? What is being done to make education accessible to all? And what is the cure for illiteracy? [2]

247

Photo: Augusto Rosales

At the UN Millennium General Assembly of 2000, the countries of the world convened to establish the Millennium Development Goals, or "MDGs," they unreservedly included, as one of the goals, universal access to primary education. In doing so, they were reaffirming the Convention on the Rights of the Child: "Make primary education compulsory and available free to all." The numbers of children excluded range somewhere between 105 and 120 million worldwide, 44 million in Africa, about 60 percent of them girls.

Everyone agrees that primary education is the salvation of struggling societies, that every additional year of schooling - beyond providing the glorious wellspring of knowledge - brings with it the best chance for better parenting, better health, better nutrition, greater opportunity, and a direct line to economic growth. How then, is it possible that the burden of school fees in Africa bedevils school attendance to this day?

Every time I travel to Africa, I encounter orphan children who are desperate to be in school, who need friends and teachers and attention, who need one meal a day that could come from a school feeding program, who need the sense of self-worth that education could bring, who want so much to learn, and who are denied it all because the costs of schooling are prohibitive.

I remember so well speaking to children who had been through the genocide in Rwanda, speaking to children physically and emotionally scarred by the conflict in northern Uganda, speaking to children orphaned by AIDS, and when asked the question, "How can I be of help to you... what do you most want?" they would all answer in identical terms, "I want to go to school." [3]

On the Indonesian island of Java, the tropical morning is already hot as ten-year-old Anis climbs down from a bicycle-driven rickshaw on the busy street. She joins her friends as they enter school to begin grade five. Anis's mother had to quit school when she was ten, to help support her family by selling homemade tofu. She and Anis's father share a small dirt-floored home with extended family. They have scrimped and saved to pay for Anis's tuition, books and uniform. They share Anis's dream that she might one day become a doctor.

Investment in girls' education is the single most effective way to reduce poverty. Educated girls marry later. They have fewer and healthier children. They are better able to care for their children and to provide for their families and themselves. They are more likely to send their own children to school.

Discrimination against girls begins at an early age. Social customs often give preference to boys. If poor parents can't afford fees for all their children, they send their boys to school. If poor communities can't afford to build separate schools for boys and girls, they favour boys. Female children often have domestic work and responsibilities that leave little time for school. Families living with HIV/AIDS usually rely on girl children to replace sick adults.

Poverty often prevents parents from paying school fees, and buying uniforms and books. Support services for students, especially child care and safe travel, are expensive and rare. Even when girls make it to school, they often drop out, because the schools don't meet their needs. The teachers, curriculum and textbooks frequently reinforce gender stereotypes. The lack of female teachers can also make girls feel less secure. [4]

- 80 million children are currently out of school... more than half of them are girls.

- Half of out-of-school children are in Africa.

- 800 million adults are missing out on the chance of an education. Nearly 1 billion people cannot read and write, 1 in 5 of the world's adult population. Two-thirds of them are women.

- An additional 18 million teachers are needed to give all children a quality education.

- Education is a Human Right: And has been promised to all people for generations. It was enshrined in the Universal Declaration of human rights back in 1948.

- Education Empowers: A single year of schooling increases a woman's wages by 10-20%.

- Education Saves Lives: Girls and boys who complete primary school are 50% less likely to be infected with HIV/AIDS. Seven million cases of HIV/AIDS could be prevented in the next decade if every child received an education.

- The Millennium Development Goals focusing on Education:
  - Ensure that all boys and girls complete primary schooling by 2015
  - Eliminate gender disparities in primary education by 2005 and at all levels by 2015. The goal for 2005 has already been missed by 94 countries, approximately 50% of the nations recognized by the UN.

- It would cost $12 billion per year to provide quality education for all children, and to teach all adults to read and write. This amount is the same as 1% of the global military budget. This amount is less than what the world spends on potato chips each year. [5]

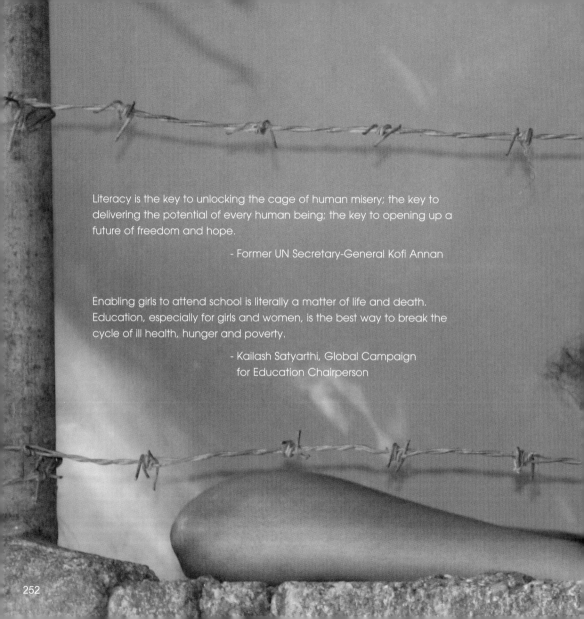

Literacy is the key to unlocking the cage of human misery; the key to delivering the potential of every human being; the key to opening up a future of freedom and hope.

- Former UN Secretary-General Kofi Annan

Enabling girls to attend school is literally a matter of life and death. Education, especially for girls and women, is the best way to break the cycle of ill health, hunger and poverty.

- Kailash Satyarthi, Global Campaign for Education Chairperson

Photo: Erin Smart

Dusty and neglected, India's poorest state of Bihar seems like the most unlikely place to encounter girl power. Yet one determined girl, Lalita, has overcome many obstacles to transform herself into an educated young woman.

Where Lalita lives, almost two-thirds of the population is living below the poverty line. Female literacy and girls' education have never been a high priority in the district. About 26 percent of female residents are literate, which is only about half the corresponding percentage for males in the district; it is also far below the state and national level.

Like many others in the village, Lalita's parents wanted her to get married at the age of 10; she only learned to read at the age of 12. Eager to learn, she secretly attended a local day school for girls from disadvantaged communities.

"I still remember the day my twin brother caught me going to school," recalls Lalita. "He beat me up since he was ashamed of the fact that I dared to study when none of the men in our family had ever attended school. My mother condoned his violence... I could not understand how mothers do not side with their daughters."

"In my village, I was doing nothing but cutting grass, fetching firewood, cleaning and cooking. In between, I used to attend school, but this was without my parents' knowledge," says Lalita. At school, Lalita and the other girls learned to read and write, and received
life skills training. They were also taught cycling, karate, hygiene, health care, and public speaking.

Lalita returned home with the skills that helped her to set up a tailoring shop. Upon her request for further education, she was sponsored in acquiring teaching skills in karate. Today Lalita travels to teach karate to girls in four schools.

"Now I believe that every daughter has the potential, and I will tell everyone to think differently," says Lalita's father, while her mother beams with pride. "Look at the respect that is being given to my daughter," says her proud mother.

Today Lalita is an independent young woman who supports herself and her family. "I want to keep studying and become an accomplished teacher. I want to teach girls about the world outside their experience, and I dream of a school in every village!" [6]

Photo: Stephanie Hunter

Education is the most powerful weapon
which you can use to change the world.

- Nelson Mandela

Photo: Stephanie Hunter

257

You can make a difference by your actions. You may think you are powerless, but together you can be the generation that sees every child get the education that is their right. World leaders have promised this and you must make sure they keep to it by joining together to speak with one voice. Promises to children should never be broken. You are the future of this world and can change it for the better. You can make leaders make their promises happen. Now the more difficult task begins to make the world keep its promises.

- Nelson Mandela

Photo: Augusto Rosales

Nearly 30 years of conflict in Afghanistan have taken a drastic toll on the country's education system. The well-documented Taliban expulsion of girls from government schools meant that girls risked their lives by attending clandestine underground schools.

Since 2001, a great deal of progress has been made regarding general, basic education in Afghanistan. In 2003, the right of all Afghan citizens to education was enshrined in the country' new constitution. Due to efforts of the Afghan government, Afghan civil society and the international community, enrolment jumped from an estimated 774,000 children in school in 2001 to 5.2 million children - including girls - by 2005. Despite this achievement, increasing unre. throughout the country now threatens to reverse this progress; recent threats of kidnappings and school attacks have meant that all children, especially girls, are reluctant to return to school. Access to education is not the only casualty of insecurity; the quality of children's education also suffers due to threats against teachers and administrators.

What is always striking to anyone who visits Save the Children schools is the obvious and overwhelming desire of these children to learn. The first village we visited was a returnee community - a village that had fled across the border into Pakistan during intense fighting during the Soviet occupation that had recently returned - lured by what they hoped would be a period of peace ushered in by the Taliban's fall. They returned with nothing except for a few essentials and quickly constructed homes from the same rocks and mud that their homes were built upon.

Sitting on the floor, cramped into a small space, sheltered from the summer heat and winter rains only by a tethered tent, these children WANT to learn. They have walked an hour and a half from home each way to be here. They fight for the teacher's attention when a question is asked, each one of them wanting to be the one to answer it.

"I want to be a doctor," one young girl replies when asked about her favourite subject, science In fact the majority of the girls want to be doctors or teachers - to teach the children in their villages and take care of the ailing in their communities. Statistics show that less than 4 percent of them will go on to do that. The dropout rate skyrockets for girls after the 3rd grade. [7]

Conflict puts society's most vulnerable children at terrible risk. Conflict can displace children, destroy schools and break down education systems. Without intervention, children can be denied access to good, safe schools or alternative forms of education - the means to rewrite their futures.

Good education rarely survives major conflict. Students and teachers often have to flee as school buildings are bombed or taken over by armed forces. As essential education money gets diverted towards military action, teachers' salaries dry up and materials stop reaching the schools. Many families can't afford school costs and the children themselves are more urgently needed to help out at home. As a conflict continues, the hope of going to school fades. Without help, these children may never go back to school. [8]

Photo: Augusto Rosales

Photo: Cindy Stover

"When I was younger there was lots of fighting. I used to be very frightened and wasn't allowed to go to school because I could be attacked. There was only one school and it was closed for many hours. I couldn't go out and play. There was nothing I could hope for. Since I have gone to school my life has changed. I know how to keep clean and have learned about children's rights. I have friends who play with me. Children who are educated will help by being doctors or teachers. For them, life will be good."

- Mary, 12, Southern Sudan [9]

With the right support, schools can be a refuge during conflict. A regular routine and a supportive atmosphere give children some normality and build their self-confidence and self-esteem. Good-quality education can also offer psychological support and healing, and can protect children from physical harm, exploitation and violence. Children can learn how to protect themselves with life skills such as landmine and HIV and AIDS awareness, knowledge they can then pass to their families and communities. [10]

263

She is the 45-year-old 'musahar' woman from Nepal's Udaypur District with four children and an ailing husband. Until four years ago, this pithy description constituted her only identity.

"No one ever called me by my name, which is Nemni Sada," she says. "Now I also know how to write it."

Ms. Sada belongs to the musahar caste - the name literally means 'rat eaters' - who are among the most disadvantaged groups in Nepal. They are considered 'untouchables', which in the heavily stratified Hindu caste system means they are too impure to rank as worthy beings. Prejudice defines their lives, particularly in the rural areas. They are routinely shunned, insulted, banned from temples and higher caste homes, and made to eat and drink from separate utensils in public places. Throughout her life, Ms. Sada has experienced double discrimination - she has been treated with disdain by the higher castes because she is a musahar and has been regarded as inferior by her own community because she is a woman.

Although Ms. Sada desperately needed to support her poor family, she was only occasionally allowed to seek work because women in her community are supposed to stay home. When she did work, she would typically receive two and a half kilos of unhusked rice for a full day in the fields and turn over all her earnings to her husband. Her children never attended school.

But all of that changed when she joined a Women's Cooperative. Such self-sustaining cooperatives, supported by the Nepalese Government and UNICEF, seek to empower women by teaching them about their rights and the rights of their children, giving them a voice and encouraging them to make decisions. The cooperatives foster the financial independence of their members through vocational skills training and loans.

With one such loan, Ms. Sada bought two piglets and embarked on her first entrepreneurial venture. A year later, she made a handsome profit when she sold the pigs. "I had never had so much money in my life before," she says. Money didn't just give Ms. Sada financial freedom, but also earned her the respect of other women in her community, many of whom have joined the cooperative.

"Even my brothers, who treated me with disdain earlier, now ask me for help," she notes.

These days, Ms. Sada is one of four women from disadvantaged groups who are members of the Executive Committee, where all decisions concerning the cooperative are made. She has become a role model in the musahar community, inspiring others to get into the mainstream too. Ms. Sada, who recently trained to become a birth attendant, is busy building a two-room brick house. She hopes that her elder son, now employed with a tractor service, will bring a bride and come live with her. Her elder daughter is married, and her younger daughter and son now go to school.

Ms. Sada says she has seen all her dreams come true, except for one. "I want him to study," she says, patting her shy, five-year-old son. "I want him to be the first government officer in our community." [11]

Photo: Stephanie Hunter

Carla, 11, is a cheerful and talkative fourth grader who feels fortunate to be able to go to school - just a year ago she was working all day selling cigarettes and candy in the streets and bars.

Carla was forced to go to work by family members when she was seven. Her job as a street vendor was difficult and dangerous. She had to work until four or five in the morning.

Carla made quite a few friends among the other children who frequented the streets, but she decided to stop seeing many of them when she realized they were using a drug called 'clefa'. The drug is a type of glue that users inhale, often to forget that they are cold and hungry.

In 2003, educators from a girls' residence arrived in the area where Carla was living. After meeting with Carla and hearing her story, she was invited to come and live with them. Carla is the youngest of the 20 girls who live at the residence. In the house, Carla gets up at 6 a.m., washes her clothes with friends in the courtyard and then makes breakfast. After that she heads off to school, eager to attend her favourite class - natural science. She loves learning about plants and animals.

Carla's dream is to attend university and become a teacher. She hopes to return and help the children who live alone or who are trapped on the street, and get them into school. [12]

Quality education is key to overcoming poverty in a single generation.

Conclusion

I have a new friend: his name is Beto, and he is the boss man out at the dump where I have taken a group of Hero Holiday® students everyday this week. We go to this dump to hand out groceries, to meet the Haitian refugees that are there, and to learn to see life from where they are, realizing that we are not all that different. Our dream is to be able to partner with their community to change the future for their children.

Beto rocked my world. He has kind eyes, and when he smiles, I see someone who I admire, because he has taught me about making the most out of a situation that wasn't his choice. This is where life has left him. He gives informal leadership to about 100 people who work at the dump, where they sort through bottles and collect food, making an average of one dollar per day. There are many hungry mouths to feed and life can be harsh for them. The air is stifling and dry, and the atmosphere is pungent. There are many women and children there trying to fend for their families, and many men just trying to walk with the only thing they can own, which is their dignity...

When our team brought water out to the people at the dump, Beto came under the tree to help me hand it out. I held the cups, and he pumped the fresh, clean water out for us. After a couple of cups, amidst our laughing and chatting, I glanced down and saw Beto's hand... and what was on his wrist. I stopped and looked again - I had to be sure - and then I choked back the tears that were threatening to fall...

On his wrist was a white bracelet. It said "Make Poverty History".

Yes, Beto, I agree. I will join my voice with yours. I will join my hands to the same work that you are doing to make a difference. My heart is linked with yours; we are from the same family, and I too am choosing to 'Make Poverty History'...

- Christal Earle, co-founder of Absolute Leadership Development Inc.

What Now?

It can seem completely overwhelming to read all these statistics and stories. In fact, it can seem so overwhelming that it can be hard to know where to start. The temptation is to want to bury our head in the sand, and hope that someone else will take action.

Making a difference starts with you, and it starts today. Advocacy is as simple as being a voice, as simple as starting with personal choices. The following pages contain some of the organizations that have been quoted within this book, and they are all making a discernible difference around the world. Please consider adding your voice to theirs, and even your support.

As was stated in this book, education is the first key to eliminating the evils of poverty and exploitation. There are many amazing resources available online and in printed form to begin to educate yourself with. Now that you are aware you have a responsibility to act. Many of the organizations listed on the following pages have email updates and even volunteer opportunities. There are also many links on the website for Absolute Leadership Development: www.absolute.org. These links are tangible ways to begin to make a difference.

Secondly, consider your everyday choices: where you shop, how you invest, and where you put your effort and focus. Are your consumer habits contributing to the continued exploitation in the global community? Are your investments ethical and advancing the cause of global equity? There are many amazing fairly traded products and companies that exist in the world, and by adding your voice and dollars to theirs, you are making the difference.

Why not experience the power of personal change by taking a Hero Holiday® or any number of other travel opportunities to make a difference in the developing world? There are numerous charities, organizations, NGO's, and churches that provide opportunities such as this throughout the year. By joining up and adding a helping hand, your life can make a lasting impact in the life of those less fortunate.

You can be the one to bring the change!

"The only thing necessary for the triumph of evil is for good men to do nothing".

- Edmund Burke

Absolute Leadership Development, Inc.

Founded in 2000 by Vaden and Christal Earle, Absolute is a federally registered not-for-profit organization based in Hamilton, Ontario. From taking hundreds of students to engage in humanitarian relief work, to presenting a message of hope to hundreds of thousands of high school students, Absolute continues to stay true to their core objective: to empower the emerging generation to change their world by living their lives with purpose. Through highly energetic school motivational presentations, volunteer-led chat lines, the Absolute School of Leadership, and numerous Hero Holiday® trips, Absolute is leaving an indelible mark on Canadian youth.

Each year, hundreds of thousands of high school students experience an Absolute Motivational Presentation. During these presentations, students encounter a captivating mix of live performers, personal real-life stories from engaging speakers, and hear about what is going on in the global community and how to make a difference.

For further information on Absolute's programs and how to get involved, to book an Absolute Motivational Experience, or to book Vaden or Christal Earle, please visit our website: www.absolute.org or call 1-866-432-4464.

Hero Holiday®

Hero Holiday® is a program run by Absolute Leadership Development Inc. We believe that this generation of youth has the capacity to affect change on the earth. Throughout the year, we provide opportunities for high school students and adult leaders to participate in humanitarian relief projects by bringing practical assistance to those living in extreme poverty. Activities may include building homes, distributing supplies, providing food, mobile medical clinics and working with children at risk. This program allows them to see first-hand how two-thirds of the world lives, expands their worldview and gives them an opportunity to become educators on world poverty by sharing their experiences. Each year, hundreds of students and adults come together to make a lasting impact on communities and individual lives. In the process, they themselves experience the most incredible transformation: the shift in perspective as they realize that they are a valuable part of the global community.

To find out more about Hero Holiday® please go to www.heroholiday.com. Make a difference. Gain a global perspective. Take a Hero Holiday®!

The Hugs Project

A HUG is an amazing thing! A 'Hug' is a tangible way for people to participate in humanitarian efforts, and more specifically, the humanitarian efforts of Hero Holiday®. A 'Hug' can be purchased for $10, and is a one-time gift that is not subject to any administration fees. A 'Hug' purchase goes directly towards the various projects that Hero Holiday® develops in the target countries of the corresponding year.

People are encouraged to purchase as many HUGS as they can, but the price will remain the same per HUG. Upon completion of each Hero Holiday® project, a summary (containing photos and testimonials) will be emailed to each HUG participant.

This email will also contain the announcement of the upcoming year's project and the opportunity to pre-purchase HUGS.

If you would like to join our efforts and use the 'Hugs' Program to raise money for a Hero Holiday® project, please contact us at www.absolute.org or call 1-866-432-4464.

Great Organizations

A lot of the stories in this book were hard to read, and a lot of the statistics seemed insurmountable. However, the point of this book has not been to make you despair or feel powerless. I don't want you to feel guilty for leading a privileged, Western lifestyle. I want you to be excited because you are in the incredible position to be able to affect change in the world. My hope is that once you've become aware of what's going on in the world around you, the choice to lead an ordinary life will no longer be an option. The following are a few organizations to get involved with that I wholeheartedly believe are actively changing the world.

World Vision
World Vision is a Christian relief, development, and advocacy organization dedicated to working with children, families and communities to overcome poverty and injustice. Through child sponsorship, World Vision addresses the immediate and long-term needs of each sponsored girl or boy. By working together with local staff and community leaders to create healthy environments and hopeful futures, children and their families are provided with things like education, skills training, nutritious food, agricultural assistance, safe water, and health care.
To sponsor a child, please visit www.worldvision.ca.

The Stephen Lewis Foundation
Stephen Lewis' work with the United Nations spans more than two decades, and the Stephen Lewis Foundation was created to help ease the pain of HIV/AIDS in Africa. This is accomplished by funding grassroots projects that help individuals, families and communities who have been ravaged by the pandemic. It provides care to women who are ill and struggling to survive, so that their lives can be free from pain, humiliation and indignity; assists orphans and other AIDS-affected children in every possible way, from the payment of school fees to the provision of food; supports heroic grandmothers, who bury their own children and almost single-handedly care for their orphan grandchildren; and supports associations of people living with HIV/AIDS, courageous men and women who have openly declared their status.
For more information, please visit www.stephenlewisfoundation.org.

Be A Hero
Led by founders Wesley and Stacey Campbell, Be A HERO is an international charity working to raise up an Army of Heroes for an urgent global crisis - endangered children. Our vision is to show others how they can help the 1.2 billion 'children at risk' because of poverty, child labour, slavery, homelessness, sexual exploitation, AIDS and plagues, and war. Be A HERO representatives worldwide present the plight of children at risk to hundreds of audiences, large and small, every year, supported by our offices in Canada, USA, Australia, and the Philippines.
For more information, please visit www.beahero.org.

Viva Network
Over the last ten years Viva has documented many tens of thousands of individuals and projects that are reaching out and speaking up for children at risk. With Regional Centres in Africa, Asia, Latin America and North America, Viva and its 78 associates currently support 7260 local projects, working together in 40 networks in 40 countries. Together, they are impacting 1.8 million children.
There are so many more children at risk that Viva wants to reach. Viva would love to hear from you; for more information or to find out how to give, volunteer or chat, please visit www.viva.org.

International Justice Mission
Founded in 1997, IJM began operations after a group of human rights professionals, lawyers and public officials launched an extensive study of the injustices witnessed by overseas missionaries and relief and development workers. This study, surveying more than 65 organizations and representing 40,000 overseas workers, uncovered a nearly unanimous awareness of abuses of power by police and other authorities in the communities where they served. Without the resources or expertise to confront

the abuse and to bring rescue to the victims, these overseas workers required the assistance of trained public justice professionals. Accordingly, IJM was established to help fill this void, acting as an organization that stands in the gap for victims when they are left without an advocate. IJM staff members (human rights experts, attorneys and law enforcement professionals) receive case referrals from, and work in conjunction with, other non-governmental organizations and casework alliances abroad.

For more information, please visit www.ijm.ca.

Hope for the Nations

Hope for the Nations was established in 1994 out of a deep conviction to address the needs of the most vulnerable and exploited members of our world - children. More than a rescue operation, Hope for the Nations works in partnership to see "the least of these" become tomorrow's leaders. This is accomplished by engaging in community development, poverty reduction and gender equity in areas where these issues intersect with children. Hope for the Nations values partnerships and international networks which efficiently and effectively serve Children at Risk in destitute situations around the world.

Please visit www.hopeforthenations.com for more information on how to get involved.

Spread the Net

Spread the Net was initiated by Belinda Stronach and Rick Mercer, in partnership with Professor Jeffrey D. Sachs, in order to raise awareness and help wipe out death by Malaria. The goal is to raise $5 million in three years for UNICEF to purchase and distribute 500,000 insecticide-treated bed nets at no cost to families in Liberia and Rwanda, and to educate recipients on their usage. Every $10 collected will purchase a bed net for a child in Africa - a simple, effective, inexpensive way to make a BIG difference - saving lives, one net at a time.

To donate a bed net, please visit www.spreadthenet.org.

Chab-Dai

Chab Dai is a network of more than twenty Christian organizations that are committed to ending sexual abuse and trafficking. These ministries work to address related issues through programs of prevention, restoration and reintegration. They are committed to assisting organizations to improve their capacity in technical skills, program support, organizations development, networking and staff support, as well as protecting children in communities, churches and programs, with a focus on the implementation of child protection policies and an understanding of child rights issues.

For more information, or to get involved in a project, please visit www.chabdai.org.

The Kindness Crew

Bestselling authors, corporate trainers and internationally acclaimed advocates for social change, the Kindness Crew is sparking a global revolution in kindness. From audiences at Fortune 500 Companies to entire metropolitan centres, the Crew has inspired and mobilized thousands to commit acts of community service. With expertise in creating and amplifying Corporate Social Responsibility (CSR) programs, the Crew has been featured in hundreds of leading publications such as The Globe and Mail, Maclean's and the National Post and has appeared on CNN Headline News, Good Morning America, Canada AM and CBC NewsWorld.

To contact the Kindness Crew, please visit www.extremekindness.com.

War Child Canada

War Child Canada is a registered Canadian charity dedicated to providing urgently needed humanitarian assistance to war-affected children around the world. War Child Canada helps generate awareness, support and advocacy for children's rights everywhere. They depend on the action taken by Canadians to raise awareness about their projects and the issues they confront. By getting involved with War Child Canada, you can help war-affected children across the world and work towards putting an end to the global poverty and conflict.

For more information on how to help, please visit www.warchild.ca.

Anti-Slavery International

Anti-Slavery International, founded in 1839, is the world's oldest international human rights organization and the only charity in the United Kingdom to work exclusively against slavery and related abuses. They work at local, national and international levels to eliminate the system of slavery around the world.

For more information, please visit www.antislavery.org.

Photographer Bios

Augusto Rosales

At the age of 20, Augusto moved from his birthplace of Mexico City to Toronto, Canada, where he assisted many successful photographers. He has been behind the camera since 1997, and has been influenced by respected photographers in the catalogue, commercial and editorial industries.

In 2005, Vaden and Christal Earle invited Augusto to cover the first Hero Holiday® trip to Republic. For him, it was a great honour - one that he could not resist. He also saw it as an opportunity to branch out into documentary photography with its many appeals. Photographing some of the poorest Haitian villages was difficult, and the unforgettable sights and smells of the local dump where men, women, and small children worked recycling had a powerful impact on him. The injustice and unfortunate examples of life's lottery compelled him to continue showing the world how truly forgotten the forgotten are. His second and third trips to Republic were no less challenging. However, the inspirational stories Augusto heard from the Canadian students and Hero Holiday® leaders on the trips remind him of the value of the work being done for these great people who deserve more of a chance.

Stephanie Hunter

Stephanie Hunter is an individual with a heart and an eye for children. Not just any children, but 'children at risk'. Stephanie has travelled the world in the capacity of both photographer and director of Hope For The Nations. Her travels have taken her to the heights of the Himalayas, the desert regions of Afghanistan and northern Kenya, the jungles of Borneo and to the streets and slums of the massive cities of our world.

Stephanie's photography has been featured on websites, at global conferences and in her book "On The Fragile Feet of Children". Her goal is to make the invisible child visible. To this end, she has been a great success.

Heather Bourque

Heather is a freelance photographer, based in Montreal, Quebec. Through her career in the aviation industry, Heather has been able to travel extensively and capture the world through her lens. In March 2007, she partnered with Hero Holiday® Thailand as a participant and volunteer photographer. Because of her natural abilities, her desire to express the story of what she has encountered is artfully expressed through her work.

Erin Smart

At the age of 19, Erin Smart travelled to Thailand where she encountered poverty in its true form for the first time. It was a trip that changed her life and opened her eyes to the reality of what poverty really looks like. Throughout her travels, she has been greatly touched by the children of the world and how poverty has impacted their lives. She has had the opportunity to visit orphanages and dumps and has seen children of all different races and backgrounds rising up through difficult circumstances and making the best of where they find themselves.

On her trip to Republic in 2006 with Hero Holiday®, she began to see how her interest in photography could be used to capture and convey the beauty of the people whom others have deemed unworthy. This has challenged her to see beyond the surface and to value each person as a life that has something to offer this world.

Aili Newstead

Aili Newstead is from Toronto, Ontario, and is currently attending the Photography Program at Ryerson University.

While in her last year of High School, Aili saw an Absolute Motivational Presentation, and was introduced to the Hero Holiday® program. The following summer she spent two weeks in Dominican Republic, and worked with the group to build a school and houses for the desperately poor. In her own words, Aili said that 'It was a fantastic experience that really opened my eyes to the world and made me aware of how truly connected we all are."

As a result of her experience, Aili is now using her photography and experience as a way to create awareness of the issues that are brought up in this book.

Nicole Sullivan

Nicole is from Toronto, Ontario, and is currently in the Environmental Studies Program at York University. Nicole participated in Hero Holiday® Dominican Republic 2007, and plans on participating in future opportunities. Nicole attributes her summer spent in Dominican Republic to literally changing her focus and career path. In her own words, her philosophy on life is 'joy does not come from the things we have but the people we are inside and the lives we touch.'

Nicole is in the process of starting a magazine for her university that focuses on social issues and poses solutions that individuals can do to change the world.

Justine Armstrong

Justine first took up photography in college, as an art expression. She has been involved with Absolute Leadership Development as a member of our High School teams, as well as being a valuable part of Hero Holiday® trips to Dominican Republic. During her time in Dominican Republic, Justine experienced a new passion and challenge to communicate the stories of the children she met through her photographs.

Justine is based out of Halifax, Nova Scotia, and is currently pursuing her dream of creating a Fair-Trade Cafe and Co-op for social justice.

Cindy Stover

Cindy has been involved with Absolute Leadership Development for two years, and she finds great inspiration in seeing students live their lives with purpose. She has been a valuable member of our High School Teams, office support and student leadership programs. She has also been greatly impacted by her participation on various Hero Holiday® trips, which have been integral in changing her perspective on social justice. Cindy is dedicated to seeing poverty and exploitation eradicated in our world.

All photographers can be contacted through www.absolute.org

Citations

Chapter 1
1. Anti-Slavery International. Visit www.antislavery.org.
2. Viva Network - Global March Against Child Labour - July 11, 2001. Visit www.viva.org.
3. International Justice Mission. Visit www.ijm.org.
4. World Vision. Visit www.worldvision.org.
5. International Labour Organization. Visit www.ilo.org.
6, 7. Anti-Slavery International. Visit www.antislavery.org.
8. BBC News. 'Chocolate Companies Blamed for Slave Labour," May 4th, 2001. Visit news.bbc.co.uk.
9. Anti-Slavery International. Visit www.antislavery.org.
10. Wesley Campbell and Stephen Court. Be A Hero: The Battle for Mercy and Social Justice. Destiny Image Publishers, Shippensburg, 2004. Visit www.beahero.org.
11. Anti-Slavery International. Visit www.antislavery.org.
12. Global March Against Child Labour. Visit www.globalmarch.org.
13. Kevin Bales. Disposable People: New Slavery in the Global Economy. University of California Press, Berkley: 1999. Visit www.freetheslaves.net.
14, 15. Anti-Slavery International. Visit www.antislavery.org.
16, 17. Labour Unity. The Bonded Labour System Abolition Act. Geneva, 27-31 May 2002. Visit www.labourunity.org.
18 . National Labor Committee. 'Wal-Mart Dungeon in China, Qin Shi Handbag Factory.' Visit www.nlcnet.org.

Chapter 2
1, 2. Source: Poverty.com. Visit www.poverty.com.
3, 4. Bread for the World. 'Are We On Track To End Hunger? The 2004 Hunger Report' Visit www.bread.org.
5. Wesley Campbell and Stephen Court. Be A Hero: The Battle for Mercy and Social Justice. Destiny Image Publishers, Shippensburg, 2004. Visit www.beahero.org.
6, 7. Bread for the World. 'Are We On Track To End Hunger? The 2004 Hunger Report' Visit www.bread.org.
8. Doris Weismann. 2006 Global Hunger Index: A Basis for Cross-Country Comparisons.International Food Policy Research Institute. Visit www.ifpri.org.

Chapter 3
1. Anti-Slavery International. Visit www.antislavery.org.
2. Ross A. MacInnes, Children in the Game; Child Prostitution - Strategies for Recovery, 1998.
3, 4. Anti-Slavery International. Visit www.antislavery.org.
5. The World Revolution. 'Human Trafficking.' Visit www.worldrevolution.org.
6. Anti-Slavery International. Visit www.antislavery.org.
7. International Labour Organization. Visit www.ilo.org.
8, 9. UNICEF. Visit www.unicef.org.
10. U.S. State Department estimate. Visit www.state.gov and montevideo.usembassy.gov
11. UNICEF. Visit www.unicef.org.
12. Jessica Williams. 50 Facts That Should Change the World. Icon Books: Cambridge, 2004.
13. Susan McClelland. 'Child-Sex Trade Thriving in Cambodia.' Maclean's Magazine: November 24, 2003. Visit www.macleans.ca.
14. United States Department of Justice. Operation Avalanche Press Conference. August 8, 2001. Visit www.usdoj.gov.
15. Newsweek Magazine, 2000. Visit www.newsweek.com.
16. UNICEF. Visit www.unicef.org.
17. CNN International. Visit http://edition.cnn.com.
18. The Straits Times (Singapore) Interactive, Sunday, July 16, 2000. Visit www.straitstimes.com.
19. Anti-Slavery International. Visit www.antislavery.org.

Chapter 4
1. Save the Children Fund. Visit www.savethechildren.org.
2. BBC News - Wednesday, 27 November, 2002. Visit news.bbc.co.uk.
3. The United Nations. Visit www.un.org.
4. Union of International Associates. Visit www.diversitas.org.
5. The Viva Network. Visit www.viva.org.
6. World Vision. Visit www.worldvision.org.
7. Paul Myhill, Journal Entry, July 02, 2007. Visit http://abandoned-orphaned.typepad.com/paulmyhill.
8. UNICEF. Visit www.unicef.org.
9. Stephanie Nolen. 28 Stories of AIDS in Africa. Alfred. A. Knopf Canada: Toronto, 2007. Visit www.28stories.com.
10. Contributed by Chipo Baloyi, as told to Patrick Makokoro, Project Development Officer for Mercy Corps Zimbabwe. Posted on Global Envision: January 31, 2006. Visit www.globalenvision.org.

Chapter 5
1. Adapted from 'Death Stalks a Continent,' by Johanna McGeary. Time Magazine, 2001. Visit www.time.com
2. Nelson Mandela. 'Care, Support and Destigmatization.' Closing Statements at the XIV International AIDS Conference, Barcelona, Spain: July 12, 2002. Visit www.nelsonmandela.org.
3. Jesse Helms - United States Senator - 'We Cannot Turn Away," The Washington Post. March 24, 2002. Visit www.washingtonpost.com.
4. On The Move - Speech by Bono at The National Prayer Breakfast in Washington, DC, 2006. Visit www.one.org.
5. Jeffrey Sachs and Sonia Ehrlich Sachs. "AIDS and Africa: Where is the US?" The Boston Globe, 2002. Visit www.boston.com/news/globe/.
6 . Stephen Lewis, Former UN Special Envoy for HIV/AIDS in Africa, at the Canadian launch of the "Make Poverty History" campaign, February 11th, 2005. Visit www.stephenlewisfoundation.org.
7. Sources: Joint United Nations Program on HIV/AIDS (UNAIDS), World Health Organization (WHO). Visit www.unaids.org and www.who.int.
8. Tim McGirk and Susan Jakes. 'Stalking A Killer.' Time Magazine: September 23, 2002. Visit www.time.com.
9. Children on the Brink 2002: A Joint Report on Orphan Estimates and Program Strategies. U.S. Agency for International Development. Visit www.usaid.gov.
10. Stephanie Nolen. "Lesotho's painfully slow fight to treat HIV." The Globe and Mail, April 6, 2006. Visit www.theglobeandmail.com.
11. Stephanie Nolen. 28 Stories of AIDS in Africa. Alfred. A. Knopf Canada: Toronto, 2007. Visit www.28stories.com.
12. Stephen Lewis. Race Against Time. House of Anansi Press: Toronto, 2005. Visit www.stephenlewisfoundation.org.

Chapter 6
1. BBC News. Visit http://news.bbc.co.uk.
2. UNICEF. Visit www.unicef.org
3. Center for Defense Information, "The Invisible Soldiers: Child Combatants," The Defense Monitor, July 1997. Visit www.cdi.org.
4. The United Nations. 'Child Soldier's Stories.' Visit www.un.org.
5, 6. Don Cheadle and John Prendergast, Not On Our Watch: The Mission to End Genocide in Darfur and Beyond. Hyperion, New York: 2007. Visit www.notonourwatchproject.org.
7, 8. Médecins Sans Frontières. 'Iraq: Let the World Know What is Happening.' September 25, 2007. Visit www.msf.org.
9. Jessica Williams. 50 Facts That Should Change the World. Icon Books: Cambridge, 2004.
10. R. Semeniuk. "War Babies." Equinox, No. 79, February 1995.
11. Jessica Williams. 50 Facts That Should Change the World. Icon Books: Cambridge, 2004.

12. Médecins Sans Frontières. 'Iraq: Surgical assistance for victims of war.' September 26, 2007. Visit www.msf.org.
13. Jessica Williams. 50 Facts That Should Change the World. Icon Books: Cambridge, 2004.

Chapter 7
1. United Nations Special Session on Children. Visit www.unicef.org.
2. Refugees International. Visit www.refugeesinternational.org.
3. European Parliament Committee on Civil Liberties, Justice and Home Affairs. 'Seminar on Prevention of Statelessness and Protection of Stateless Persons within the European Union.' June 26, 2007. Visit www.europarl.europa.eu.
4, 5. The UN Refugee Agency. Visit www.unhcr.org.
6, 8. Refugees International. Visit www.refugeesinternational.org.
9. Sojurn House. 'Refugee Stories.' Visit www.sojournhouse.org.
10. BBC News. 'A Refugee's Story: Torn Apart." Visit news.bbc.co.uk

Chapter 8
1. Wesley Campbell and Stephen Court. Be A Hero: The Battle for Mercy and Social Justice.
Destiny Image Publishers, Shippensburg, 2004. Visit www.beahero.org.
2, 3. Source: UNICEF. Visit Visit www.unicef.org.
4. Source: World Health Organization, (WHO). Visit www.who.org.
5. Sources: UNICEF Visit www.unicef.org, American Red Cross Visit www.redcross.org, World Health Organization (WHO) Visit www.who.org.
6, 7. World Health Organization, (WHO). Visit www.who.org, UNICEF. Visit www.unicef.org.
8. CBC News. 'Thousands of children still dying daily from preventable diseases: report.' February 22, 2006. Visit www.cbc.ca .
9. Sources: UNICEF, World Health Organization, (WHO). Visit www.who.org. Rehydration Project.Visit http://rehydrate.org.
10. Sources: World Health Organization, (WHO). Visit www.who.org. Stop TB Partnership. Visit www.stoptb.org.
11. Source: Debt, Aids, Trade Africa. Visit www.data.org.
12. Sources: World Health Organization, (WHO). Visit www.who.org. Stop TB Partnership. Visit www.stoptb.org.
13. Spread the Net: Bednets Against Malaria. Visit www.spreadthenet.org.
14. Sources: World Health Organization, (WHO). Visit www.who.org, UNICEF. Visit www.unicef.org.
15, 16. Spread the Net: Bednets Against Malaria. Visit www.spreadthenet.org.
17. Debt, Aids, Trade Africa. Visit www.data.org.
18. UNICEF. Visit www.unicef.org.
19. The Canadian International Development Agency. Visit www.acdi-cida.gc.ca.
20. Wesley Campbell and Stephen Court. Be A Hero: The Battle for Mercy and Social Justice. Destiny Image Publishers, Shippensburg, 2004. Visit www.beahero.org.
21. Suzanna Dayne. 'Going the extra mile: UNICEF Indonesia immunization drive reaches remote areas.' Visit www.unicef.org.
22. Celia W. Dugger. 'Preventable Disease Blinds Poor in Third World.' The New York Times. March 31, 2006. Visit www.nytimes.com.
23. CBC News. 'Thousands of children still dying daily from preventable diseases: report.' February 22, 2006. Visit www.cbc.ca.
24. Reported by Margaret Lowrie. 'Red Cross warns of threat from preventable diseases.' June 28, 2000. Visit www.cnn.com.

Chapter 9
1. U.N. Wire, July 23, 2004. As reported in the 2005 edition of State of the World, published by The Worldwatch Institute. Visit www.worldwatch.org.
2 -11. UNICEF. Visit www.unicef.org.

Chapter 10
1. Wesley Campbell and Stephen Court. Be A Hero: The Battle for Mercy and Social Justice. Destiny Image Publishers, Shippensburg, 2004. Visit www.beahero.org.
2. Huguette LaBelle, Chair, Transparency International. '2007 Corruption Perceptions Index.' London, September 26, 2007. Visit www.transparency.org.
3. Stephen Lewis. Race Against Time. House of Anansi Press: Toronto, 2005. Visit www.stephenlewisfoundation.org.
4. Wesley Campbell and Stephen Court. Be A Hero: The Battle for Mercy and Social Justice. Destiny Image Publishers, Shippensburg, 2004. Visit www.beahero.org.
5. International Justice Mission. Visit www.ijm.org.
6, 7. Global Witness/Amnesty International US Diamond Retail Survey 2007. Visit www.amnestyusa.org.
8. Interview with Victor Malarek, author of 'The Natashas: Inside the New Global Sex Trade.' February 7th, 2006. Visit www.pbd.org.
9. Wesley Campbell and Stephen Court. Be A Hero: The Battle for Mercy and Social Justice. Destiny Image Publishers,Shippensburg, 2004. Visit www.beahero.org.
10. Stephen Lewis. Race Against Time. House of Anansi Press: Toronto, 2005. Visit www.stephenlewisfoundation.org.

Chapter 11
1. The Canadian Global Campaign for Education. Visit www.campaignforeducationcanada.org.
2. Morgan Kirk. 'The Right to Education.' Relevant Media Group. Visit www.relevantmagazine.com.
3. Stephen Lewis. Race Against Time. House of Anansi Press: Toronto, 2005. Visit www.stephenlewisfoundation.org.
4. The Canadian International Developmeny Agency. Visit www.acdi-cida.gc.ca.
5. The Canadian Global Campaign for Education. Visit www.campaignforeducationcanada.org.
6. UNICEF. Visit www.unicef.org.
7. Jiffer Bourguignon. 'An Introduction to Rewrite the Future in Afghanistan.' Save the Children, December 2006. Visit www.savethechildren.ca.
8, 10. Save the Children Canada. Visit www.savethechildren.ca.
11, 12. UNICEF. Visit www.unicef.org.

How to Order Copies

To Order more copies of One, or to inquire about wholesale pricing for using this book as a charitable fundraiser,
please visit **www.absolute.org**. To book a speaking engagement with Vaden Earle,
please call **1-866-432-4464**, or visit our website.

Get Started Helping Your World

LOVEGLOBAL by Darian Kovacs
An outline for helping people start a community volunteer, global thinking, environmental club.
This booklet has been designed to answer the question:
What can I practically do to help my world?

ISBN: 0-9737279-2-6

To purchase LOVEGLOBAL and other student resources check out www.campusfire.com/store

FRIESEN ENVIROLUX

ENVIRONMENTAL BENEFIT STATEMENT

One project saved the following resources by printing
this book on Friesen Envirolux paper made with 80% recycled fiber, 40% post-consumer
waste and processed chlorine free.

trees	water	energy	solid waste	greenhouse gases
43	15,531	29	2,570	4,738
fully grown	gallons	million BTUs	pounds	pounds

Calculation based on research by Environmental Defense and other members of the Paper Task Force.

Friesens is pioneering environmentally friendly alternatives for school yearbooks.

PONDER PUBLISHING

Friesens
The Yearbook Company

Printed in Canada
on Acid-Free Paper